MW00332784

Open Ark Series Volume 1

Maggie's Legacy

Lessons in Spiritual Obedience Learned from My Border Collie

SALLIE DAWKINS

Reviews

When Sallie Dawkins set out to get a pet for her child, she didn't realize it would be the beginning of an eight-year spiritual journey that would completely change her outlook on life. God used a beautiful border collie named Maggie to open the author's eyes to aspects of worship and meditation she took for granted. – Essien A. for Readers' Favorite

Dawkins utilizes her interaction with the dog to illustrate God's unfailing love for us and how He may communicate with us via the seemingly trivial things in our everyday lives. – Adanna O. for Readers' Favorite

Maggie's Legacy was written with compassion and offers a wealth of practical exercises to help readers grow in spiritual understanding. This book's life-changing lessons will guide pet lovers into a deeper connection with God. Highly recommended! – Theodora Higgenbotham, M.Ed, and Author of *Lies, Secrecy, and Deception Unlocked*

Maggie's Legacy is a delightful series of stories about a beautiful border collie and Sallie who loves her. Maggie listens to Sallie, and Sallie listens to God. If you are a dog lover, you'll be blessed by this book. – Janet H., Reader Review

I adore how the author guides us through the journey with her dog, highlighting how she overcame the challenges they experienced while never letting us forget God's lessons. *Maggie's Legacy* is a book I'd suggest to any Christian who wants to deepen their faith. – A. Ora for Readers' Favorite

Maggie's Legacy may be a book about a dog, but it reads more like a daily devotional manual. Each chapter ends with a section of soul-searching questions allowing the readers to introspect, providing a spiritual panacea for those who feel lost in their journey. When you combine that with the history and care tips for a border collie, you get a dose of spiritual enlightenment unlike any other. – E. Asian for Readers' Favorite

Maggie's Legacy: Lessons in Spiritual Obedience Learned from My Border Collie

The Open Ark™ Series, Volume 1

Library of Congress Control Number: 2022922940

eBook ISBN: 978-1-955861-43-4; Print Paperback ISBN: 978-1-955861-44-1

Copyright © 2022 by Sallie Dawkins

All rights reserved. Except for brief quotations in printed reviews, no part of this publication may be reproduced, stored in a retrieval system, or transmitted in any form by any means (printed, electronic, audio, digital, or otherwise) without the prior written permission of the publisher. Exclusive use of all images reserved (C) 1995-2022 Sallie Dawkins and Firebrand United, LLC. Duplication is expressly prohibited.

All views and opinions represented in this book belong solely to the author. Some names and places have been changed to preserve privacy. This publication is a source of valuable spiritual insight and information for born-again Christians; however, it is not meant as a substitute for God's word. No part of the author's words, views, or opinions should supersede God's word.

Although the author and publisher have made every effort to ensure that this book's information was correct at press time, they do not assume and hereby disclaim any liability to any party for any loss, damage, or disruption caused by errors or omissions. The information in this book does not replace or substitute professional advice in financial, medical, psychological, or legal matters. You alone are responsible and accountable for your decisions, actions, and results in life. References are provided for informational purposes only and do not make up endorsements of any kind.

Endnotes have been auto-generated by Atticus. Readers should know the websites and links listed in this book may change.

Please note that Firebrand United's publishing style capitalizes pronouns that refer to God. This may differ from some publishers' styles.

All Scripture quotations are sourced from www.BibleGateway.com. Scripture credits are noted at the back of the book under "Bible Translations." Unless otherwise noted, italics and brackets within quotes are maintained from the source.

Experience God's love through the Open Ark™ Series' heartwarming true stories about animals, shared by the humans who love them.

Names: Dawkins, Sallie, author.

Title: Maggie's legacy : lessons in spiritual obedience learned from my border collie / Sallie Dawkins.

Series: Open Ark

Description: Danville, KY: Firebrand United, LLC, 2022.

Identifiers: LCCN: 2022922940 | ISBN: 978-1-955861-44-1 (paperback) | 978-1-955861-43-4 (ebook)

Subjects: LCSH Christian life. | Dogs--Religious aspects--Christianity. | Border collie--Training. | BISAC RELIGION / Christian Living / Spiritual Growth | RELIGION / Inspirational | PETS / Dogs / Breeds | PETS / Dogs / Training

Classification: LCC BV4501.2 .D39 2022 | DDC 242--dc23

Published by
Firebrand United, LLC
PO Box 2506
Danville, KY
40423-2506 USA
www.FirebrandUnited.com

Contents

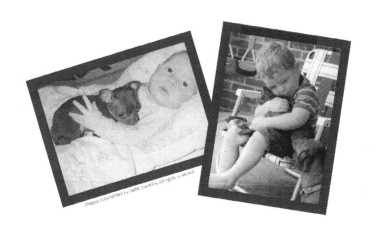

Images copyrighted by Sallie Hawkins. All rights reserved.

I dedicate this book to Creator God and all the animal friends You sent to teach us to love.

"Just ask the animals, and they will teach you. Ask the birds of the sky, and they will tell you."

Job 12:7 (NLT)

Introduction

Dogs have been a part of our family for as long as I can remember. However, God's hand was on it when we adopted a rather ordinary Border Collie-Corgi mix puppy from a local rescue shelter. Our Maggie was a super-smart, long-haired black beauty with short legs and big brown expressive eyes.

God will bless and use whatever we hold in our hands if we release it to Him. As Maggie's primary caregiver, I had a dog on a leash. In God's hands, she became a valuable tool for ministering healing to me and many others. Pets are not people, but they can be wonderful, loyal companions who enrich our lives in unexpected ways. They're an undeniably important part of our families. I never imagined that God could use a dog to teach me, but that's what He did.

Maggie wasn't instantly skilled at leash-walking, and I wasn't immediately adept at prayer walking. We learned how to work it out together. Walking the dog helped shut off all the mind-chatter and allowed me to see my surroundings differently. Through Maggie, I learned God was interested in the minor details of my life, and I could call on Him anytime.

Just as Maggie learned to follow my directions, step by step, I was learning to follow the guidance and direction of the Holy Spirit. Over time, it became clear that Maggie and I were on a parallel training path. Maggie's corrections were often lessons of reflection for me as well, and as Maggie matured, I did, too.

God's unconventional methods of teaching memorable life-lessons challenged my thinking. If God was teaching me so much through my interactions with a dog, how much more was He speaking in other areas of my life, through other ordinary things that I had missed? If God would use a dog in supernatural ways, how much more would He use me?

I believe God is always talking to us; He is the "Word," after all. I invite you to read **The Awakening Christian Series** if this concept is new. It's my testimony of growing in identity, potential, and purpose in Christ. Volume 1 of this series, *You Can Hear the Voice of God through All Your Spiritual Senses*, answers common questions Christians ask about the many ways God speaks.

When hearing God's voice was new to me, I learned to ask Him to validate His words with scripture. This simple act proved valuable. As God directed me back to scripture, I fell in love with the Bible and grew to depend on His faithful nature and character.

Whether individually, with your family, or as a small group, it's fun to use the stories as conversation starters to talk with God. You'll also find "Questions for Prayer or Journaling" at the end of each chapter. Many new Christians find journal prompts helpful. Prayer is part of our ongoing dialogue with God, and journaling helps us focus on these important conversations.

I invite you to apply the lessons from these encounters to your own life. More than feel-good dog stories, this book is a collection of revelatory life lessons, words of correction, and encouragement that God has shared with me over the past few years. Each story stands on its own, making this book ideal for busy pet lovers and Christians everywhere.

God's love and blessings to you. Always.

Sallie

Image copyrighted by Sallie Dawkins. All rights reserved.

Chapter One

Adoption Day

It had been five years since our precious Prissy died. A gift from my mom, Prissy, came to us as a tiny, one-pound Chihuahua. That same year, I was married, started grad school, moved three times, left a full-time job, and had a baby. Prissy survived it all!

At just five pounds fully grown, this little dog with a big personality was with us for twelve wonderful years. I grieved when Prissy started showing signs of distress and held her as she took her last breath.

Our children were now older and busy with work and school. With the house's increasing quietness, the Lord softened my heart to consider getting a puppy. I don't think we even talked about it at first, but one day I was compelled to look online to see what kinds of dogs might be available for adoption locally.

The search lasted for weeks. One online search led us to a little Dachshund named Sam. That afternoon, my youngest son and I visited the local animal shelter. Although Sam was probably a wonderful dog, he didn't seem like a good fit for us. We discovered he was older than advertised and didn't respond well to people or toys. He was also incredibly yappy- I didn't know if I could handle all that yapping!

Glancing around, I noticed a woman coming in from the parking lot. A trusting puppy snuggly clung to her shoulder. "We should have a dog like that," I whispered to my son.

We had already walked through the holding pen area once, but I agreed to walk through again before leaving. Animal adoption facilities often have similar features. The "holding pens" were dog runs. A "dog run" is a fenced-off area that keeps animals safely separated while allowing indoor-outdoor access.

In this building, there must have been twenty or more pens facing each other with a narrow walkway between them. Eager dogs jumped up on the wire-gated doors, and their barks echoed loudly throughout the metal building. Some dogs looked scared; others looked aggressive. *Lord, I can't handle this noise,* I muttered. *Are You sure it's time for us to get a dog?*

My eyes locked on a black puppy standing upright with her paws on the gate. Her curly tail wagged wildly. If you had seen her, you probably would have thought, like I did, that her circling tail would lift her off the ground at any moment, like a helicopter taking flight. In all the commotion of that place, she was the only dog not barking. How had I missed her?

Ah, this was the snuggly puppy I saw the woman carrying earlier! A volunteer informed us that local families often temporarily fostered younger animals. Foster families were committed to providing interim care for animals. They returned the animals to the facility for regularly scheduled community-wide adoption events.

The attendant shared more details as she read from a chart retrieved from the filing cabinet behind the reception desk. We discovered the puppy was a five-month-old Border Collie-Corgi mix. Her name was Maggie. The woman I saw carrying her from the parking lot was her foster mom. Locking eyes with my son, we both grinned. Through hope-filled smiles, we immediately asked if Maggie could join us in the outdoor play area.

Intelligent and playful, quiet and engaging, Maggie was perfect for our family. We completed the forms and paid the required fees, officially adopting her. Perhaps I hadn't thought things through before leaving the house that afternoon. "Going to look at a dog" and "adopting a dog" were two very different processes. Unprepared, we loaded Maggie into the car, then rushed to the store to purchase puppy supplies—a crate, bed, toys, and food.

Initially, we thought Maggie would be a delightful companion for our youngest son. However, with him being in school most of the day, she quickly attached herself to me. Maggie responded well to everyone, and there were no hard feelings. It was the beginning of a season of instruction and lifelong friendship for all of us. We learned many things from and through Maggie, perhaps none more than me.

Looking back, it's clear that God softened my heart and prompted me to look online for a dog. I was still very immature in my faith, even though I had been a Christian for over twenty years. I honestly thought I believed in God. Still, I wavered in my faith walk because I wasn't entirely convinced of His love.

When we adopted Maggie, we agreed to be her forever family. We wouldn't have considered returning her to the shelter. She was ours, and we were hers. Similarly, the Spirit of adoption (also sometimes referred to as the Spirit of sonship) comes with eternal love when we come to salvation through Christ Jesus (Romans 8:15).

God's tool for teaching me about Kingdom perspective, obedience, and purpose came through my everyday interactions with Maggie and, most often, through ordinary dog walks. Isn't that just like God? When I thought I was training Maggie, the Lord was teaching me! Through this relationship, I learned God is always speaking and will use ordinary things in our life to reveal profound truths. God is never far from us and provides for our needs at just the right time!

Image copyrighted by Sallie Dawkins. All rights reserved.

Scriptures to Ponder

"Before I formed you in the womb, I knew you. Before you were born, I sanctified you. I have appointed you a prophet to the nations." (Jeremiah 1:5 WEB)

...that he might redeem those who were under the law, that we might receive the adoption as children. (Galatians 4:5 WEB)

...having predestined us for adoption as children through Jesus Christ to himself, according to the good pleasure of his desire, (Ephesians 1:5 WEB)

For you didn't receive the spirit of bondage again to fear, but you received the Spirit of adoption, by whom we cry, "Abba! Father!" (Romans 8:15 WEB)

... but God chose the foolish things of the world that he might put to shame those who are wise. God chose the weak things of the world that he might put to shame the things that are strong. (1 Corinthians 1:27 WEB)

Questions for Prayer or Journaling

Pets touch our hearts in beautiful ways. Do you have any pets? What is your pet's name?

Do you recall when your pet was born or adopted into your family? Do you remember the day you believed and received salvation to be adopted into God's family?

Share one thing that makes your pet unique. Now ask God to share one thing that makes you special to Him. Listen and make a note of His response.

Let's Pray

Father God, thank You for Your loving kindness toward us. Thank You for the Spirit of adoption that allows us to be called Your sons and daughters. We don't have to jump up and down or make loud noises to get Your attention; Your eye is always on us. You know just what we need, exactly when we need it. Thank You for the special pet friends You have sent to help us learn from You. Open the eyes of our hearts to see Your fingerprints in all things. In Jesus' name, amen.

Image copyrighted by Sallie Dawkins. All rights reserved.

Chapter Two

Open Hearts Open Doors

I never cease to marvel at how God builds bridges using ordinary things. Babies in strollers and puppies on leashes seem to have a special anointing for opening doors and hearts.

After twelve years of living in the same house, I had good relationships with neighbors to the left and right. Still, a miracle happened when Maggie became a part of our family. For the first time, we were walking through the neighborhood. Neighbors working in their yards would wave to us. Children would ask all about Maggie. "What's your puppy's name?" "Can I pat your puppy?" "How old is she?" "Does she do any tricks?"

Our new acquaintances shared freely about their pets, either past or present. As Maggie matured, our walks grew longer, and our territory expanded. Neighbors with pets would invite us to play in their backyards or join them on walks. We also learned their stories. Neighbors like Bob and Joe had lived side-by-side for over forty years. Though I didn't know, they had watched my children grow up. We'd walk past their houses on the way to school. Yet it wasn't until Maggie came along that we officially met. Not only did our Christmas card list grow, neighbors opened their doors to allow us to pray.

Our neighbor, Sherry, didn't attend church but believed in God. One day, as Maggie and I were walking past her house, we noticed her sitting on the front steps outside. Stopping to visit, Sherry shared she was experiencing extreme pain in her arm and shoulder and might need surgery. I immediately offered to pray. Did God free her from that pain? He sure did! He's still in the business of doing miracles! It not only built Sherry's faith, but it also increased mine, too! From then on, Sherry would invite me to join her in praying for the needs of her friends or family.

God is genuinely interested in every part of our lives. Not only were people smiling, waving, and sharing stories, lasting friendships grew out of these encounters. God used Maggie to connect members of our community, even after years of disassociation. Opening their hearts to a puppy on a leash also opened doors for ministry!

Image copyrighted by Sallie Dawkins. All rights reserved.

Scriptures to Ponder

Even so, let your light shine before men, that they may see your good works and glorify your Father who is in heaven. (Matthew 5:16 WEB)

As you would like people to do to you, do exactly so to them. (Luke 6:31 WEB)

For the whole law is fulfilled in one word, in this: "You shall love your neighbor as yourself." (Galatians 5:14 WEB)

So then, as we have opportunity, let's do what is good toward all men, and especially toward those who are of the household of the faith. (Galatians 6:10 WEB)

Questions for Prayer or Journaling

Have you met your neighbors? What are some ways you might connect with others in your community?

Do you have a testimony of healing or other miracles? Invite God to remind you of His presence in your life.

We used to teach our children, "if you want to have a friend, be a friend." In what ways could you be a friend to others in your neighborhood? Has God placed a burning desire in your heart to serve others?

Let's Pray

Father God, we celebrate You! You are brilliant! You use babies and puppies to draw people together. Lord, grant wisdom, uncommon sense, and an increase in the discerning of spirits (1 Corinthians 12:10) to protect us from all harm as we learn to step out in faith to connect with others. Burden our hearts to pray for all Your sons and daughters everywhere. Use us to lead others to Jesus as You pour out Your Spirit of Salvation upon all the earth. In Jesus' name, amen.

Chapter Three

"Don't be 'That' dog."

One evening, while Maggie and I were walking along the paved path of a busy local park, God spoke unusually. I sensed He had a lot to say about the dogs we encountered. Although He pointed out the dog's apparent behaviors, His words weren't meant to condemn but to teach.

See that dog leaning hard on the leash? He's stretched as far as the leash might go but wants to sniff something beyond his reach. He's tilted sideways with his total weight on the harness and leash. He's a bossy little one who doesn't understand boundaries or limits. Don't be that dog.

See that little dog? The owner is walking, but the little dog is getting dragged along. The owner says, Yes. The dog says, No. He's fearful, untrusting, defiant, and overly pampered. Don't be that dog.

See that dog? He's so happy when his owner asks, 'Who wants to go for a walk?' He jumps up and down in excitement. He's everywhere all at once, jumping up on people walking by. Now he's dragging his owner around, going after every squirrel, bird, rabbit, or bug. Then he has to pee on absolutely everything. Can you hear him? "This is mine. It's mine. This is mine, too." He's selfish and easily distracted. Don't be that dog.

See that dog? He thinks he owns the sidewalk, but he's wearing a choke collar. He growls and barks at everyone. He's scary, unfriendly, and hostile. Don't be that dog.

Which dog, Lord? I asked.

Be the dog who walks nicely with a slack leash, in step with the Owner, watching as he's walking, ready for the following command. Be the friendly, engaged, correctable, trusting dog that stops when the Owner says, "Wait." You must be willing to be trained and grow in loyalty. Be a friend to the Master and a joy to be around. Be that dog.

I don't know if the Lord was speaking to Maggie, but He was definitely speaking to me! He'd illustrated His point well, and I understood how His words could apply to my life. God is always speaking if we know His words and ways. As Ambassadors of Christ, we represent the Kingdom of heaven on earth. Our attitudes, thoughts, comments, and actions reflect our beliefs about God, ourselves, and others. Another valuable reminder from our ever-present God.

Scriptures to Ponder

"...but this thing I commanded them, saying, 'Listen to my voice, and I will be your God, and you shall be my people. Walk in all the way that I command you, that it may be well with you.'" (Jeremiah 7:23 WEB)

"Why do you call me, 'Lord, Lord,' and don't do the things which I say?" (Luke 6:46 WEB)

"If you love me, keep my commandments." (John 14:15 WEB)

Therefore prepare your minds for action. Be sober, and set your hope fully on the grace that will be brought to you at the revelation of Jesus Christ— as children of obedience, not conforming yourselves according to your former lusts as in your ignorance, (1 Peter 1:13-14 WEB)

Questions for Prayer or Journaling

Why is it important for Christians to represent Christ well? Who are you influencing? Do your words and actions draw others closer to Christ or repel them away from Him?

Which dog's behavior stood out to you the most, and why? What is God speaking to you through this?

The dogs we encountered at the park that day seemed well-loved and cared for by their owners. Trainers help improve behavior by evaluating a dog's behavior, then working with the family to create a training plan. Positive reinforcement seems to be the easiest method for changing a dog's behavior. According to Romans 2:4, the goodness of God leads men to repentance. How does this verse apply to your life?

We grow in awareness of God's faithful presence as we grow in spiritual maturity. When we know God's Word and ways, we see Him everywhere! What are some of the unique ways He communicates with you?

Let's Pray

Father God, thank You for Your daily corrections. A picture is truly worth a thousand words. Lord, forgive us for acts of resistance and stubborn rebellion. Your insights instill the fear of the Lord to bring true wisdom, shedding revelation light, and bringing radiant healing. Open the ears of our hearts to listen to Your advice carefully. In Jesus' name, we pray. Amen.

Chapter Four

Frisbee Foolishness

E ven the best pets can challenge us sometimes. When Maggie stopped eating food from her bowl in the kitchen, but devoured the same food served from her Frisbee, it made me question things!

Maggie loved her little pink squeaky ball and would carry it around in her mouth, prepared for sudden invitations to play fetch, but she loved her Frisbee the most. Frisbee was her BFF (best friend forever), with whom she shared all her secrets and happy times. In the mornings, when she'd sit at the back door surveying the yard, it was Frisbee she'd run to first.

Digging her teeth into Frisbee's familiar rim, Maggie pranced around the yard's edges, looking like a pony in a circus show. She wanted Frisbee to see what she was seeing, stopping only to flip Frisbee into the air with the fanfare of a graduation cap on graduation day. Maggie and Frisbee played this game in the backyard for hours.

Maggie could hardly stand to be told no, so she'd sometimes let Frisbee ask the questions. Tossing Frisbee at my feet during office hours was an invitation to play. Who could say no to Frisbee?

Flying is what Frisbee did best. Outdoors, Maggie would circle in the opposite direction to get a running start before skillfully twisting her body to leap several feet into the air. Sea World's™ bottle-nosed dolphins had nothing on Maggie!

Maggie would scoot Frisbee across the hardwood floors inside the house with her nose. Periodically she'd use her teeth to toss him into the air, but Frisbee was a wildcard. When he'd had enough, he'd roll under the sofa to rest. Perhaps my most important job was to reach my long arms under the couch to retrieve him. Maggie and Frisbee's indoor games on the hardwood floor were loud and intense, echoing through the entire house, but Maggie loved it, and I loved Maggie.

Maggie had the same food and water bowls from when she was a puppy, so I don't know what caused her to decide she no longer wanted to eat her food from the bowl. When one day turned into two, I grew concerned.

Frisbee was always nearby, so not even thinking, I just flipped him over and filled him with Maggie's kibbles. The same food rejected from her bowl garnered circle tail wags and enthusiastic jumping when served from Frisbee. Was it more than friendship, a matter of presentation, or boredom?

One day, I took the matter to God. "Lord, here we have a perfectly good bowl, yet Maggie won't use it! What's going on?" His response brought conviction.

In my spirit, I heard the Lord say, *Here we have a perfectly good Bible- the Holy and inspired Word of God, yet you won't sit with that. You'd rather have it filtered through the current best-selling author. You love how it's re-packaged and re-stated. You rely on men's words rather than God's Word. You look to men to help you grow rather than relying on the Holy Spirit.*

Ouch! Truth pierces the heart, and the sting of conviction is sharp. Indeed, the hungry are satisfied with God (Psalm 146:7 TPT), but those without understanding feast on foolishness (Proverbs 15:14 TPT). The Bible will always be our primary source for learning from God (Matthew 6:33); supplemental resources like books or podcasts serve a secondary purpose.

After a while, Maggie grew tired of having her food served in Frisbee and transitioned back to eating meals from her bowl. Although Maggie eventually outgrew this phase, she and Frisbee maintained their bonds of closeness. And me? God's corrections drew me nearer to Him. Cutting off the teaching and prophetic voices of others for an extended period led me straight back to my first love (Revelation 2:4-5).

A Frisbee is not a food bowl, and men's teachings can't take the place of God. The supernatural love, comfort, wisdom, and revelation we require to navigate this world can only come from God.

However, it's precious to lead friends into His presence.

Image copyrighted by Sallie Dawkins. All rights reserved.

Scriptures to Ponder

But seek first God's Kingdom and his righteousness; and all these things will be given to you as well. (Matthew 6:33 WEB)

But solid food is for the mature, whose spiritual senses perceive heavenly matters. And they have been adequately trained by what they've experienced to emerge with understanding of the difference between what is truly excellent and what is evil and harmful. (Hebrews 5:14 TPT)

Every Scripture is God-breathed and profitable for teaching, for reproof, for correction, and for instruction in righteousness, (2 Timothy 3:16 WEB)

As for you, the anointing which you received from him remains in you, and you don't need for anyone to teach you. But as his anointing teaches you concerning all things, and is true, and is no lie, and even as it taught you, you will remain in him. (1 John 2:27 WEB)

Questions for Prayer or Journaling

Invite God to reveal any areas of your life where you lean on men rather than Him.

No matter how often I read the Bible, I still learn new things. When was the last time you invited God to direct your reading for the day?

Sometimes we're tempted to adopt certain scriptures as truth and discard other scriptures as expired. Yet, the entirety of God's Word is eternal. Ask the Lord if you have wrongly rejected Him, or parts of His Word, by accepting doctrines of men or denominations without question.

Let's Pray

Father God, empower us to seek You with all our heart, soul, mind, and strength. Expose the enemy's deceptions. Grant wisdom and discernment to know when we are foolishly following the ways of this world. We desire to live in the confidence and boldness of Your glorious love. Thank You for inviting us to feast on the truth of Your Word. We praise You, Lord, for You alone bring peace to our borders. It's in the brilliant name of Jesus we pray. Amen.

Chapter Five

Longsuffering

Having come to Christ as an adult, I still vividly recall the time I naively prayed for patience as I waited on the resolution of a drawn-out legal issue. God promptly responded to my request by allowing me to wait six years for the conclusion of that matter. With this experience to look back on, I can say with complete certainty that I would likely never have prayed for anything related to that concept ever again. Who would, right?

Does anyone wake up in the morning thinking, *Today seems like the perfect day to pray for longsuffering!* Never! But that's what I did. Surely, God placed it on my heart to pray for longsuffering. I likely wouldn't have prayed for it otherwise! *Longsuffering* means suffering through something for a long time. We can also define it as patiently enduring a long-lasting offense or hardship, being slow to anger, or not being provoked easily.

Sometimes when we pray, it takes a while to get an answer. Other times, we get results rather quickly. When I prayed for longsuffering, the Lord responded almost immediately with an opportunity to have my patience tried. As usual, the lesson came through Maggie.

We had worked on proper leash-walking for years, and it didn't happen overnight. But this day, it tried my patience as Maggie had to stop every three feet. Why? Why did she need to sniff everything that every other animal had ever stepped on or peed on for the *entire* walk?

I wanted to walk but was tempted to cut our outing short and return home. I wanted to go from *here* to *there* and return home as quickly as possible. I had work to do, and these invisible distractions messed with my schedule. One of the significant benefits of working from home is that you're no longer trapped in rush hour traffic, but that's how it felt.

Stop.

Go.

Stop.

Go.

Stop.

Somewhere along the way of stopping and starting, my thoughts turned to God, and I wondered if I ever behaved this way with Him. God often wants to take us on a journey from Point A to Point B, and it's not that far to go, but we get so easily distracted. Do we stop every few steps along the way?

Do we start a task, then a second task, or maybe even another? Some days (or seasons), it can be a real toss-up to see if we'll ever go back to finish any of those things we've started. Are we tempted to pack things up and walk away from them altogether? Doing so would be an inefficient use of time.

Unnecessary delays are not the only negative consequence of worldly distractions. As frustration builds, a seed of ingratitude can take root. If we're not careful, we'll soon find ourselves mumbling, grumbling, whining, and complaining. We see this happen with the Israelites who left Egypt to enter the Promised Land. Because of their sins, the original forty-day journey took forty years (Numbers 14:34). Yet we know God was with them every step.

Dear reader, no part of our journey takes God by surprise. He sees everything and loves us so much that He's willing to longsuffer with us. Through it all, He remains faithful to His nature, patiently moving us forward in His mercy, grace, and love.

Investing time with God always produces a good return. The enemy attempts to interrupt our time with distractions to cause us to lose focus on the one thing that matters most—God.

When random thoughts threaten to interrupt my prayer time, I take them captive by jotting them down (2 Corinthians 10:5, Philippians 2:5). While *What's for dinner?* and *Is it time to change the oil in the car?* are essential questions, I don't want to be consumed with these thoughts during my time with God. When thoughts demand to be heard and shift into a cycle of repeating, making a note of them in the margins of my journal frees me to stay focused on God's Word and presence.

In Psalm 27:4, David says the one thing he's asked of God is to allow him to dwell in Yahweh's house all the days of his life. David was a man after God's heart and was intent and content to seek after God all the days of his life.

Maggie's stop-and-go behavior was a sweet reminder of God's endearing love. It also caused me to consider how I might be more intentional in my pursuit of Him.

Scriptures to Ponder

But the fruit of the Spirit is love, joy, peace, longsuffering, gentleness, goodness, faith... (Galatians 5:22 KJV)

I therefore, the prisoner in the Lord, beg you to walk worthily of the calling with which you were called, with all lowliness and humility, with patience, bearing with one another in love, being eager to keep the unity of the Spirit in the bond of peace. (Ephesians 4:1-3 WEB)

Count it all joy, my brothers, when you fall into various temptations, knowing that the testing of your faith produces endurance. Let endurance have its perfect work, that you may be perfect and complete, lacking in nothing. (James 1:2-4 WEB)

The Lord is not slow concerning his promise, as some count slowness; but he is patient with us, not wishing that anyone should perish, but that all should come to repentance. (2 Peter 3:9 WEB)

Questions for Prayer or Journaling

Do distractions sidetrack you during the day? In what ways can you regain focus or help others stay on track?

Read Matthew 5:37. What does it mean for your yes to be yes? Invite God to remind you of anything you've started, set aside, or not yet finished. What steps would you need to take to complete these projects or tasks?

Do you have daily goals? Sitting with God at the start of each day and asking Him for wisdom brings clarity by ordering our steps. Our times are in His hands (Psalm 31:15), and He can teach us to use time more efficiently to expand the Kingdom of heaven on earth.

Habakkuk 2:2 encourages us to write the vision, make it plain, and run with it. Would your priorities change if you knew you only had only five more years to live? What if that timeframe was reduced to twenty-four hours? What changes would need to take place for you to live with no regrets?

Let's Pray

Lord God, forgive us for being slow to learn and easily distracted. Thank You for Your great patience. Teach us to always put You first in all we think, say, and do. Restore vision, helping us to keep our eyes on You. Teach us to focus. You are worthy of our full attention. There is absolutely nothing Your power cannot accomplish. You have given us the mind of Christ. Everything we need is already within us. Thank You for guiding us past the distractions of life. Pour out a finisher's anointing upon all we set our heart and hands to, for Your ways are perfect. We trust You completely. We love You and adore You. It's in the mighty name of Jesus we pray. Amen.

Chapter Six

Heart Check

As good as Maggie was, she occasionally acted like a spoiled child. Sometimes she made me think she only hung out with me because she needed someone to open the treat jars.

I don't think she fully appreciated our time playing ball outside, walking, or riding in the car. These things were not "treat" enough. As soon as we'd get back inside the house, she'd sit by the treat jar and stare at it longingly.

If I ignored her behavior, she would pace back and forth as if to create a neon sign with her body pointing the way to the treat jar. She would continually turn her gaze from my hands to the jar until I opened it. Maggie worked hard to train me!

Superficially, this behavior might seem cute or clever. Still, at a deeper level, Maggie communicated that spending time with me was not enough. Was she only interested in the treats? Eventually, she'd drop her head and walk to her crate, sulking, especially if she didn't get the treats she thought she deserved. Head down, with her big brown expressive eyes throwing sad glances from side to side, her disappointment was obvious.

I wondered if I was ever that way with God.

God's continual intercessions are for our prosperous well-being. He's with us every moment of our journey. Through His Word, he teaches, tests, and corrects. He even watches over us at night while we're sleeping. Indeed, He is a loving Father who lavishes us with many gifts. But do we treat Him as if all of this is not enough?

Are we continually asking for signs and wonders, visions and visitations, dreams, miracles, and angelic encounters?

Are we continually attempting to control or influence God? Is our attitude toward Him pure, or do we expect treats, worldly recognition, or rewards in return? Do we act as if being in His presence is not enough? Are we attempting to manipulate, bribe, or get our way? Are we focused on the treats? Do we seek after God because we love Him or because there's something in it for us?

Do we feel entitled to all "good" things because of our obedience to God? In 2 Corinthians 11:24-28, the apostle Paul shares that his obedience to Christ has led him to suffer accusations, beatings, stoning, imprisonment, shipwreck, and more. Have we allowed our hearts to grow callous with resentment because we've forgotten that God's goodness often comes packaged in suffering?

These are hard questions we must ask and answer for ourselves.

God wants us to want Him. We've sinned when we make the mistake of placing security in the blessings of God rather than in God Himself. He is more than enough! So, how can we be sure there are no hidden heart motives? We can ask Him to reveal our hearts to us. There should be no off-limit areas He cannot access.

We don't have to wonder. No need to sulk, self-isolate, or distance ourselves from God and others. A heart check is as easy as asking, "Hey, are we good? I'm asking You to let me know if there's something 'off' that we need to talk about." This works with God and people, too, since we are to love God *and* others. But when you ask, be ready to hear and receive the truth. If our motives or attitude for doing anything for God (or for others) is anything but love, we may need to repent.

Scriptures to Ponder

As for me, I said in my prosperity, "I shall never be moved." You, Yahweh, when you favored me, made my mountain stand strong; but when you hid your face, I was troubled. (Psalm 30:6-7 WEB)

Search me, God, and know my heart. Try me, and know my thoughts. (Psalm 139:23 WEB)

Every way of a man is right in his own eyes, but Yahweh weighs the hearts. (Proverbs 21:2 WEB)

For our light affliction, which is for the moment, works for us more and more exceedingly an eternal weight of glory, while we don't look at the things which are seen, but at the things which are not seen. For the things which are seen are temporal, but the things which are not seen are eternal. (2 Corinthians 4:17-18, WEB)

You ask, and don't receive, because you ask with wrong motives, so that you may spend it on your pleasures. (James 4:3 WEB)

Questions for Prayer or Journaling

Pray and ask God to search your heart's motives, thoughts, and attitudes. Allow Him to shine His light of love on your heart and soul.

Do you keep a gratitude journal? I challenge you to note three things you are grateful for daily and share that list with an accountability partner.

We don't want to take God's loving kindness for granted. When was the last time you thanked Him for His presence in your life?

How should we respond when the Holy Spirit corrects us for spoiled, entitled, or prideful attitudes or ways?

Let's Pray

Father God, we owe You so much. We never want to take You for granted. It's our joy to spend time with You. We delight in Your presence. Lord, we ask Your forgiveness for the times we have dishonored You by failing to show proper reverence and respect. Lord, we're sorry for the times we came to You hard-hearted and empty-handed. You deserve our very best. You are our Lord and Master, our Beloved Bridegroom King. You alone are worthy of all praise. In Jesus' name, amen.

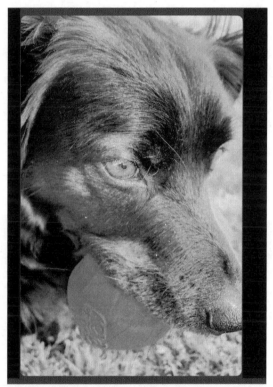

Image copyrighted by Sallie Dawkins. All rights reserved.

Chapter Seven

Growing in Maturity

When Maggie was brand new to our family, she was a bundle of energy! She had the sweetest disposition, but all that puppy excitement soon wore us out! We wanted Maggie to feel welcome and loved, but clearly, we had forgotten the basics of communicating with dogs. Recognizing that we needed help establishing clear boundaries and realistic expectations, we scheduled an in-home visit with a local dog trainer.

Each breed of dog is known for specific traits and temperaments. Maggie was our family's first Border Collie. We soon learned Collies are highly intelligent, active, working dogs who need a lot of space for running and herding. Hiring a dog trainer was one of the best investments we ever made.

Hope for a brighter future came as Maggie responded to the trainer's directions quickly and effortlessly. We learned that consistency with commands, routines, and redirections would be crucial to Maggie's success. The trainer showed us just a glimpse of what Maggie was capable of, but in our eyes, she was brilliant!

None of this changed the fact that Maggie had high-octane puppy energy for almost three years! Indoors, she frequently bounced off people and furniture, and a fenced-in yard offered a reprieve from her constant need to run at full throttle. Her resistance to learning the art of leash-walking left me crying tears of frustration on more than one occasion.

Yet, on this day, as we walked our familiar route through the neighborhood, God drew my attention to how nice she was walking and reminded me of her growth. Indeed, she hardly seemed like the same dog! Now almost five years old, I trusted Maggie to walk obediently by my side, with or without a leash.

That same morning, we encountered an older gentleman walking a brown and white Border Collie puppy. We heard them coming from far off. The man spoke loudly as he roughly handled the puppy, snatching it from side to side. It was a curious and alarming sight to behold.

We stayed the course, greeting them as they approached. As the man shared his story, my eyes remained on the beautiful puppy. Honestly, she could have bolted out into oncoming traffic at any moment. She was a six-month-old high-energy, headstrong girl who loved jumping and twisting herself on the leash. Her name was Maizy, and she was more unpredictable than an atomic bouncing ball in a small room. The man's name was Tom, and he quickly let me know this wasn't *his* dog. Maizy belonged to his wife, and he wasn't happy about shouldering all the responsibility for the dog's care.

Maizy wore a metal choke-collar, and Tom had a large pouch of treats fastened to his belt. It seemed he was prepared for anything--negative consequences and positive reinforcements. I wondered what his expectations were.

Tom shared he was retired, but his wife was still working, so caring for the puppy during the day was entirely his responsibility. Maizy always wanted to play fetch-the-ball, and Tom was tired of walking her three times a day. Recalling that Maggie had started the same way, I suggested a trainer might help.

Tom said Maizy had been to three different trainers already; and that his wife sometimes took her to doggy day-care so that she could be around other dogs. He confessed that his real frustration was that he never wanted a dog, and now he had to take care of this puppy while his wife did other things. Tom had grown to resent the entire situation.

Maizy was only doing what puppies do. She was a handful, but Tom seemed more frustrated with his wife not listening than he was with the dog's unacceptable behavior. Isn't it funny how people are sometimes more comfortable venting and sharing their deepest thoughts and feelings with total strangers rather than the people closest to them? Tom needed to have this conversation with his wife so the two of them could work on a solution together.

This encounter reminded me that poor communication and false, unrealistic, or unmet expectations could cause a lot of frustration. Frustration can lead to resentment; resentment can lead to bitterness, and that's not a good road to travel.

Communication involves exchanging information, and it's not just about talking; it also involves active listening. Over time, and with consistent training, guidance, redirection, and correction, Maggie matured into a loyal, obedient, and trustworthy dog.

Reflecting on Maggie's growth caused me to consider how I, too, had matured. When I was new to prayer, I didn't await God's answers. Does God expect us to get everything right as soon as we receive salvation? While some people may experience immediate, profound changes when they come to Christ, it doesn't happen that way for everyone. It didn't happen that way for me.

Still, we shouldn't stay baby Christians forever. My spiritual immaturity showed when I had one-sided conversations with God where I voiced my needs through prayer, along with exactly how, and when, I'd like Him to respond. When we pray, we communicate with our Lord and King, and God desires us to love and trust Him.

Even when I was resistant and rebelled against God, His love for me was steadfast. He never once threw up His hands in frustration or disgust towards my wrong beliefs and behaviors. God doesn't use choke-collar restraint methods, but He allows us to experience the consequences of our poor choices and negative behaviors.

When we fall, fail, or make messes or mistakes, God does not grumble, condemn, threaten, or change His mind about us. Instead, His plan for change consists of radical love and heart-to-heart encounters. Jesus paid the price for the world's sins, including all of my sins, not just part of them (1 John 2:2). There's nothing left for me to work out or earn. When I receive the Truth of His Word and His eternal, unconditional love, I grow in spiritual maturity and prosper in all things.

Pets are a great responsibility, but they enrich our lives immensely. When God called us to host ministry in our home, Maggie's presence brought joy, love, and healing. When people met Maggie, they saw a well-trained dog obedient to her caregiver. She didn't stay a boisterous, disobedient puppy. She matured, but it was a process that happened gradually, requiring commitment and consistency. Similarly, when people meet me, I hope they see someone growing in spiritual maturity (Ephesians 4:13-14).

We don't have to be like anyone else. Though we may have similar traits or beliefs as Christians, we're each uniquely created in God's image and likeness. Holy Spirit is the best Trainer! God never changes His mind about us—He's rock-solid committed in our relationship, and we can be, too!

Scriptures to Ponder

If I give everything I own to the poor and even go to the stake to be burned as a martyr, but I don't love, I've gotten nowhere. So, no matter what I say, what I believe, and what I do, I'm bankrupt without love. Love never gives up. Love cares more for others than for self. Love doesn't want what it doesn't have. (1 Corinthians 13:3-7 MSG)

Now, if anyone is enfolded into Christ, he has become an entirely new creation. All that is related to the old order has vanished. Behold, everything is fresh and new. (2 Corinthians 5:17 TPT)

These grace ministries will function until we all attain oneness in the faith, until we all experience the fullness of what it means to know the Son of God, and finally we become one perfect man with the full dimensions of spiritual maturity and fully developed in the abundance of Christ. And then our immaturity will end! And we will not be easily shaken by trouble, nor led astray by novel teachings or by the false doctrines of deceivers who teach clever lies. (Ephesians 4:13-14 TPT)

Questions for Prayer or Journaling

Are there any areas of unrealistic expectation or frustration in your life? If so, this might be an area God wants to touch. You can choose to give these frustrations over to God. How? First, repent for holding on to unforgiveness; then ask God to bless the person, business, or situation. Invite Him to give you wisdom and understanding in that area. Ask, "Lord, how do you see this situation? What would You like to see happen here?"

When you pray, do you expect God to respond? Are you intentional about spending time with God and asking Him how you can minister to Him, or allow Him to minister to others through you?

What would God think about your maturity? Are there noticeable areas of spiritual growth and maturity in your life? Partnering with more mature, like-minded Christians can help you grow in spiritual maturity. Do you have spiritual mothers or fathers to help you with accountability? If you're already walking in a measure of spiritual maturity, do you have spiritual children in your life?

Let's Pray

Father God, thank You for always being with us and never giving up on us, even in awkward stages. Help us, Lord, to trust You more in every area of our lives. Holy Spirit, help us see as You see. Teach us always to see the best in everything and everyone. Thank You for guiding us into the fullness of spiritual maturity and showering us with Christ's abundant love. Thank You for being Lord over every area of our lives. In the mighty name of Jesus, we pray. Amen.

Chapter Eight

Forgetting What She Once Knew

We employed a family friend to stay at our house to pet-sit Maggie during an extended absence. Everything went well, but somehow during our week apart, Maggie un-trained herself to use the doggy door.

I don't know how she forgot how to use the doggy door, but upon our return, I soon found myself coaxing her with, "You can do it!" "Come on!" "Push the door open!" "You've got this!" There I was, clapping, cheering, and offering treats to help Maggie recall what she once knew. Still, her retraining took time.

Through it all, we never yelled at her. We didn't remind her of the past, saying, "You used to know how to do this. What's wrong with you, stupid dog?" We didn't withhold our love from her until she learned to get it right. These passive-aggressive kinds of responses are not effective with people or pets.

Rather than threaten, yell, punish, or instill pain or fear, it's best to honor life and nourish connections. We weren't mad at Maggie; we accepted the situation for what it was. Animals respond well to positive reinforcement, and we started over from one step back. Somehow, she had forgotten the mechanics of using the doggy door. As we retrained, we celebrated the baby steps she got right. Not "again," but right then.

We might find a similar un-learning process in our own lives occasionally. New Christians who've been in church for a short period might think they can skip attending church a few times. Doing so can lead to the temptation of quitting church altogether. This doesn't just apply to church attendance. We can all get out of the habit or "forget" to make time for prayer, study, praise, or spending time with God.

We need to stay connected with God, and that's often easier to do with believers who will hold us accountable. Perhaps you've noticed someone absent from church activities this week. Don't assume someone else will reach out. Why don't you call, text, leave a message, write a note or send a card? Let them know they're missed.

Checking on friends and loved ones to ensure they're okay makes them feel valued. Perhaps they need help. That person absent from church is your brother or sister in Christ. They're in your life for a reason and are vital to the proper functioning of the body of Christ. Plus, they're incredibly important to God!

If loved ones have walked away from God, continue praying for restoration. There's no need to judge or bring up the past. Just evaluate the new starting line and go from there. Cheer them on, encourage them, and love them. We can win others over to Christ more effectively by showing them Christ's love, not preaching to them all the time.

With guidance and encouragement, Maggie soon learned how to use the doggy door again. If you're ever in a position where you forget what you once knew, it doesn't mean all is lost. It feels good to know others haven't given up on us and will walk alongside us to recover lost ground.

Image copyrighted by Sallie Dawkins. All rights reserved.

Scriptures to Ponder

Day by day, continuing steadfastly with one accord in the temple, and breaking bread at home, they took their food with gladness and singleness of heart, (Acts 2:46 WEB)

Let's consider how to provoke one another to love and good works, not forsaking our own assembling together, as the custom of some is, but exhorting one another, and so much the more as you see the Day approaching. (Hebrews 10:24-25 WEB)

...looking to Jesus, the author and perfecter of faith, who for the joy that was set before him endured the cross, despising its shame, and has sat down at the right hand of the throne of God. (Hebrews 12:2 WEB)

But if we walk in the light, as he is in the light, we have fellowship with one another, and the blood of Jesus Christ, his Son, cleanses us from all sin. (1 John 1:7 WEB)

Questions for Prayer or Journaling

According to Proverbs 11:25, "those who refresh others will themselves be refreshed" (NLT). Ask God to use you to encourage someone today.

When you were a new Christian, did you feel the overwhelming love of God? Invite Him to restore you to your First Love.

Suppose you're feeling disconnected in your relationship with God or others. What are some steps you could take to move toward reconnection? How can you be a friend to others? What are some ways you can share God's love with others?

If sharing God's love with others is a topic that interests you, you might enjoy *You Can Share the Love of God with Others,* Book 3 of The Awakening Christian Series.

Let's Pray

Father God, You remember Your covenant with us. You will never forget us. Lord, forgive us for ignoring the truth of Your word and choosing to believe lies instead. Train us up again. Strengthen us to stand firm in faith. Teach us to speak in a way that echoes Your eternal love and shines a clarion light to this dark world in which we live. In Jesus' name, amen.

Image copyrighted by Sallie Dawkins. All rights reserved.

Chapter Nine

"I'm glad you let me carry you."

Maggie was subject to more frequent baths than most dogs because of a family member's ongoing allergies. Symptoms of allergies included itchy eyes, sneezing, and contact dermatitis resulting in hives. When these symptoms manifested, Maggie and all her bedding would get washed.

Her favorite blanket was a hand-knotted red throw with colorful ladybug designs. Wherever the blanket went, Maggie was sure to go. Therefore, you can understand her concern for the blanket getting tossed into the washer; and her ultimate relief when the dryer's signal let out a loud *BUZZ!* When the dryer door opened, Maggie would retrieve her clean and warm "blankie," restoring it to its proper place within her crate.

On hot summer days, we might wash Maggie in the backyard with the water hose, but most often, she'd have a bath in the tub upstairs. To limit allergen exposure in the sleeping areas, the upstairs of our home was off-limits to pets. The exception to this rule was when Maggie needed a bath.

The job of washing Maggie was almost exclusively mine. I learned the best way to carry a wiggly twenty-five-pound puppy up the stairs was to sit on the bottom step, lightly patting my lap while calling her name. We used this particular hand signal only for bath time. Though Maggie sometimes came forward rather sheepishly, she ultimately responded by climbing onto my lap.

From this seated position, I'd wrap my arms around her body, stand, then carry her up the stairs to the hallway bath. I often imagined this might be the same way a shepherd carried a lamb. Once upstairs, I'd kneel to place her gently in the tub where we used a hand-held shower sprayer to wash her.

Maggie could have wiggled, squirmed, or fought the whole time, but she never did. She trusted me and remained calm. On our way upstairs one day, I whispered to Maggie, "I'm so glad you let me carry you."

Something about that day was different, though. As soon as I spoke those words aloud, I could hear God repeating that phrase straight back to my spirit.

Sallie, I'm so glad you let me carry you.

I replied aloud, "Lord, I'm going to let You carry me any time you want to."

I've already been carrying you, came Holy Spirit's response.

"Oh. Well, in that case, thank You for carrying me."

Thank you for letting Me.

I didn't always let God carry me. That's hard to confess, but I'm sure others realized. People who have unprocessed trauma often throw up walls as boundaries. Attempts to control people or situations are fear-based reactions. I operated from self-reliance for decades because I didn't trust God or others to help. It seemed easier to do things myself rather than risk possible rejection or further failed attempts to communicate my needs to others.

Ongoing difficulties caused me to feel like I was drowning, and everyday anxieties left me gasping for air. Though my arms weren't literally flailing, it often felt like I couldn't get a grip on anything, and I just wanted someone to throw me a life jacket. On the inside, it felt like no one cared or heard me, but my feelings weren't accurate.

God is always with us. He has said He will never leave or forsake us (Deuteronomy 31:6). Psalm 22:24 of The Passion Translation says, "...he has not despised my cries of deep despair. He's my first responder to my sufferings, and he didn't look the other way when I was in pain."

Perhaps I had gotten so used to everything being a struggle that I didn't realize I was standing in shallow water and could stand up at any moment. Viewing the world and people through the cracked lenses of past wounds caused me to perceive the world as unsafe and unwelcoming.

Acting and reacting according to how things might have been in my past kept me from moving forward on my healing journey. Rather than fighting the shallow water, I might have given up the unnecessary wrestling and stopped struggling with situations and those closest to me. How different life became when I stopped lashing out to resist the ones God sent to help heal, purify, mature, and build my faith.

I've learned that when I grow weary from the battles of life, I can trust God to carry me. He's an expert at navigating crossovers. Just as Maggie trusted me with washing her favorite blanket and taking her up the stairs for bath time, we can also trust God to carry us through life. He's a good Father who enjoys holding His children close, and we can relax and risk being vulnerable with Him.

One encounter with the King of Love can heal the most profound soul wounds. He is our covenant-keeping all-sufficient Savior who preserves our life according to His Word (Psalm 119:37) and restores us to vibrant health. He will not let us drown in the circumstances of this world (Isaiah 43:2). With God, we can stand on the solid ground of His Word or relax and enjoy floating.

Image copyrighted by Sallie Dawkins. All rights reserved.

Scriptures to Ponder

"...and in the wilderness where you have seen how that Yahweh your God carried you, as a man carries his son, in all the way that you went, until you came to this place." (Deuteronomy 1:31 WEB)

When you pass through the waters, I will be with you, and through the rivers, they will not overflow you. When you walk through the fire, you will not be burned, and flame will not scorch you. (Isaiah 43:2 WEB)

"For I, Yahweh your God, will hold your right hand, saying to you, 'Don't be afraid. I will help you.'" (Isaiah 41:13 WEB)

"Even to old age I am he, and even to gray hairs I will carry you. I have made, and I will bear. Yes, I will carry, and will deliver." (Isaiah 46:3-4 WEB)

In all their affliction he was afflicted, and the angel of his presence saved them. In his love and in his pity he redeemed them. He bore them, and carried them all the days of old. (Isaiah 63:9 WEB)

Questions for Prayer or Journaling

Have you ever felt like you were drowning in your circumstances? How did you recover from that experience?

Journal and ask, "Lord, are there any areas of my life where I'm resisting Your willingness to carry me?"

Trying to carry burdens God never meant for us can leave us heavy and weary. In Matthew 11:30, Jesus tells us His yoke is easy, and His burden is light. Ask God if there's anything you need to release to Him today. Are there any false burdens you've been bearing? Now might be a good time to "leave it" with the Lord!

Let's Pray

Father God, I will trust in You. The tests and trials of this life purify my heart, yet You don't leave me to navigate this realm alone. You have given me Your Spirit of Holiness as my Counselor, Comforter, and Guide. You are intimately aware of me, Lord, perceiving every movement of my heart and soul. Wherever I go, Your hand guides me, and Your strength empowers me. See if there is any path of unnecessary pain I'm walking on, and lead me back to Your glorious, everlasting ways (Psalm 139:24 TPT). In Jesus' name, amen.

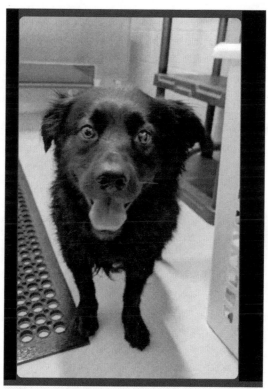

Image copyrighted by Sallie Dawkins. All rights reserved.

Chapter Ten

From Where Does My Help Come?

B order Collies have thick double coats, so during the summer months, Maggie and I preferred to walk through the neighborhood early in the morning or late at night. On this day, we were making our rounds close to midnight.

Following well-lit neighborhood sidewalks was usually uneventful, but on this night, we soon approached a large mound of old carpet and padding discarded by a local homeowner. Recent heavy rains had caused this massive hunk of rubbish to move, which now obstructed our path.

Everything was fine until Maggie spotted this colossal mess. We'd walked that same route thousands of times without incident. Suddenly faced with an unfolding eyesore, Maggie's reaction to the unfamiliar obstacle caused me to question my response to unforeseen roadblocks.

Maggie kept walking, though she moved at a slightly slower pace. She communicated her concerns by glancing at that soggy disarray of carpet, then turning sharply to make eye contact with me as if to ask, *Do you see this? What are we going to do about this?* She was watching my reaction and awaiting directions on how to proceed.

It made me wonder, *Do I respond that way in my walk with God?*

If it weren't for Maggie, I wouldn't be outside, walking around the neighborhood near midnight. During the years we lived pet-free, I never felt the urge to walk alone to pray through the community. Yet, walking with Maggie made this seem the most natural thing in the world.

Long walks with Maggie offered good exercise for both of us, and I learned to use those times for talking with God. Some days, I'd pray or sing in my prayer language. My words often flowed between an unknown tongue (Acts 10:46), or prayer language, and native English effortlessly. I don't know how she did it, but Maggie knew the difference between me praying and talking to her. Maggie consistently discerned the contrast between the two and accurately followed directions every time.

As Maggie looked to me for guidance in navigating this obstacle on this late-night walk, I assured her, "It's okay; you're safe." We sidestepped that enormous mass of carpet by taking a slight detour into the yard.

On the other side of that mess, I said, "Good job, Maggie. You're so brave." I praised her for listening and following directions. She got a treat when we got home.

Do we let some obstacles bend us all out of sorts, wondering and worrying how we're going to handle these new things like we have to deal with them alone? Are we tempted to give up when we face life's hindrances?

My friends, God is always with us. His perspective is more accurate than ours. Isn't He faithful and trustworthy? Listening to His directions, we continue to move forward, though it might seem slower than usual.

God blesses us because He wants to, not because we performed well or beg Him to hear our prayers. God delights in us and enjoys our company. And there you have it- another unexpected lesson of faith I learned from my dog.

Scriptures to Ponder

I will lift up my eyes to the hills. Where does my help come from? My help comes from Yahweh, who made heaven and earth. (Psalm 121:1-2 WEB)

Trust in Yahweh with all your heart, and don't lean on your own understanding. In all your ways acknowledge him, and he will make your paths straight. (Proverbs 3:5-6 WEB)

And your ears will hear a word behind you, saying, This is the way; walk in it, when you turn to the right hand and when you turn to the left. (Isaiah 30:21 AMPC)

... while we don't look at the things which are seen, but at the things which are not seen. For the things which are seen are temporal, but the things which are not seen are eternal. (2 Corinthians 4:18 WEB)

Questions for Prayer or Journaling

Are you faced with any unexpected obstacles in life right now? Have you asked God how He sees the circumstance or situation or the best way to navigate it?

How do you handle the temptations of falling back to self-reliance or leaning into self-righteousness?

According to Hebrews 11:6, God rewards those who seek Him. Read this verse in your favorite Bible or app. What does this verse mean to you? For additional insights, consider reading Genesis 6:8, Deuteronomy 4:40, 1 Samuel 15:22, and 2 Chronicles 27:6.

Let's Pray

Father God, You are so beautiful! We enjoy Your company and can live confidently in and from Your glorious presence. Fit our eyes with blinders as we navigate these narrow paths. Your face is ever before us; we don't need to look left or right to receive guidance or directions from this world. We are citizens of heaven. You are our God and King. Grant wisdom for leading others in a way that honors and glorifies You alone. In the matchless name of Jesus, we pray. Amen.

Image copyrighted by Sallie Dawkins. All rights reserved.

Chapter Eleven

Yuck!

Though Maggie was a great friend and valuable member of our family, her true dog nature shined one chilly November morning. A neighbor was outside clearing small sticks and debris from her yard and invited us to see how her landscaping renovation project was going. Leaves, branches, and uprooted plants littered the grounds.

When we needed to take care of things like this in our yard, we loaded up our little yard cart and moved everything into the fire pit to burn. Our dear neighbor seemed relieved when I offered to remove some of her excess branches, and it wasn't difficult.

I detached the leash from Maggie's harness while we picked up sticks. Soon, she was drawn to a pile of dried leaves and started rolling in them. *How cute*, I thought.

When the cart was full, I signaled for Maggie to "come." She obediently romped joyfully to my side. It was good to see her enjoying herself. Reattaching the leash to her harness, we headed home with the cart in tow.

After completing our outdoor chores and putting everything away, we headed inside to finish loading the morning's breakfast dishes into the dishwasher. I didn't think anything of it when Maggie walked straight to her crate to lie down. I was standing in the kitchen, gazing out the window over the sink, when I felt Maggie's familiar nudge against my leg. Instinctively reaching down to pat her head, I received an unexpected shock. Instead of the cuddly bunny-soft fur I was used to, my hand came into contact with a clump of matted, sticky hair. *What in the world is this?*

Ugh! The smell was *wretched!* Not only was it all over Maggie, but it was also now on *me!*

If this had happened two weeks earlier, I would have marched Maggie straight to the backyard and hosed her down with the water hose. However, we had just turned off the outdoor spigot for the winter as temperatures had already dropped below freezing. My only option was to carry her upstairs for a bath.

With the stench getting riper by the moment, I ran to open the back door. Eyes scanning the room, I quickly snatched up the nearest squeaky toy, tossed it outside for Maggie to follow, and closed the door behind her.

I needed time to get the bathroom ready. There was no way I would risk her rubbing any of that horrific smell on anything else in the house. It was pure *yuck!* I cannot imagine what kind of animal or fluid she had found to roll in, but it must have smelled irresistible to her!

It was no surprise when the usual gentle-formula shampoo didn't work on that monstrous stench. I quickly grabbed the Dawn™ dishwashing liquid. If this product was good enough to clean wildlife caught in oil spills, it might work on Maggie.

After finishing up the unscheduled bath, I carried Maggie downstairs for drying off and brushing.

Unfortunately, things were worse than I thought. The smell was still locked in. We hastily moved back upstairs for one more bath. I hated that Maggie smelled so bad, but how could I get mad at her for being a dog?

Although whatever she had rolled in seemed good to her, it certainly didn't seem good to me! While dog washing and laundering dog towels and bedding had not been on my schedule for the day, it quickly became my priority.

Somewhere amidst it all, I thought of our Redeemer's lovingkindness and compassion (Isaiah 54:8) towards me. Were my recent behaviors on par with Maggie's?

The Autumn and winter holidays are filled with candies and goodies. I purchased a bag of chocolate candy bars earlier in the week. Half-priced Halloween candy seemed like a good deal, but I knew chocolate and sugar were triggers for overeating.

I had one candy bar.

Then another.

And another.

I didn't try to stop. I just rolled with it. Indeed, this had been a terrible stench to God. Did it honor my body to eat like this? No. Did it glorify God? No. Did it taste good? Of course! But was it good? No.

It was not good for me. I took the matter to God, confessing to Him what He already knew, and asked His forgiveness. I repented for this and renounced the gluttony and rebellion attached to it. Then I tossed the remaining chocolate bars straight into the trash. I should never have allowed this temptation to enter my house.

If this "yuck" had stayed on Maggie, it would have prevented her from enjoying my company. On this day, Maggie's restoration required multiple baths. Similarly, through Christ, we have been made clean and restored to God (Hebrews 10:8-12).

A dog can't get clean on its own, and neither can we. We need Jesus. God used this yucky experience to remind me of His love and forgiveness. Our washing in the water of God's word (Ephesians 5:26) is continual.

Image copyrighted by Sallie Dawkins. All rights reserved.

Scriptures to Ponder

"In overflowing wrath I hid my face from you for a moment, but with everlasting loving kindness I will have mercy on you," says Yahweh your Redeemer. (Isaiah 54:8 WEB)

Therefore, since Christ suffered for us in the flesh, arm yourselves also with the same mind; for he who has suffered in the flesh has ceased from sin, that you no longer should live the rest of your time in the flesh for the lusts of men, but for the will of God. (1 Peter 4:1-2 WEB)

But each one is tempted when he is drawn away by his own lust and enticed. Then the lust, when it has conceived, bears sin. The sin, when it is full grown, produces death. Don't be deceived, my beloved brothers. (James 1:14-16 WEB)

If we confess our sins, he is faithful and righteous to forgive us the sins, and to cleanse us from all unrighteousness. (1 John 1:9 WEB)

Questions for Prayer or Journaling

Read 1 John 4:18 in your favorite Bible or app. Are you guided by fear of punishment or God's love?

When we receive salvation in Christ, we begin an ongoing sanctification process. He's already factored in all the mistakes we'll ever make. God's love for us is based on Christ's righteousness, not our own. Journal and ask God to reveal the truth of His love for you.

Sweets and chocolates used to be temptations for me. Do you have any temptations? What does God say about this topic? Read Matthew 6:13, Matthew 26:41, 1 Corinthians 10:13, and James 1:12 from your favorite Bible or app.

If given the opportunity, do you think Maggie might have run back to the neighbor's yard to roll in that yuckiness again? Proverbs 26:11 tells us a fool repeats his foolishness, just as a dog returns to its vomit. Do you feel ruled by bad habits or negative thoughts? How might you stop unfavorable or harmful cycles from operating in your life?

Let's Pray

Father God, Your goodness and love have pursued me throughout my life. I confess my failures to You, and You forgive me. In mercy, You have seen my true condition and cared for me. My life is in Your hands. When I am overwhelmed, You hear my prayers and rescue me. I am bathed in the splendor and light of Your presence (Psalm 26:8 TPT). You deliver me from the enemy's strongholds and cleanse me of all unrighteousness. Let Your love and steadfast kindness overshadow me continually (Psalm 33:22 TPT). In Jesus' name, amen.

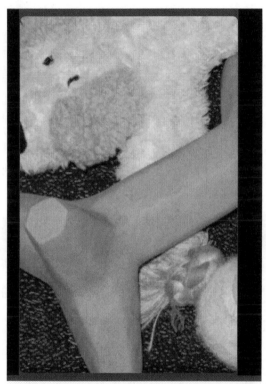

Image copyrighted by Sallie Dawkins. All rights reserved.

Chapter Twelve

When Mistakes Happen

F or many years, Maggie and I enjoyed predictable routines. Upon waking, we'd walk to the back room overlooking the deck, and I'd open the sliding glass door just wide enough for Maggie's body to pass through. Sitting in that open space with all her favorite toys nearby, she'd take inventory of any changes that might have occurred in the yard during the night.

She bolted out the door, quick as lightning, if she noticed anything amiss. Unlike her human counterpart (me), she didn't put things on her schedule for later. Once she saw an issue, she would immediately and obediently deal with it.

Over the years, Maggie developed into an excellent guard dog. She knew well the invisible boundaries of the house and yard and did not overstep those areas. If, while playing fetch, her ball fell into a neighboring yard, she'd look to me for instruction or permission to "leave it" or "get it."

The many hours and years invested in Maggie's training and reinforcement of commands resulted in a beautiful partnership. Maggie was a loyal friend, confidant, and comforter.

Maggie grew to know my expectations and the sound of my voice, spoken commands, and hand signals. Her natural affinity and willingness to learn new things made her a dependable asset for ministry, despite her shaky beginning.

When Maggie was a puppy, there were many times we grew frustrated with the training process. Still, we kept at it consistently. Even when our patience wore thin, we started each new task of the day with fresh grace. In time, Maggie exceeded the ten tricks required for certification as an AKC trick dog. While that was fun, her greatest value was as a PTSD service dog. Though there were no federal registries for service dogs then, we expected Maggie to be well-behaved in all settings.

In our home, misbehaving children might be sent to their rooms for a timeout in response to angry outbursts or temper tantrums. I learned over time I needed the timeout more than anyone else. Retreating to my bedroom's quiet, dark space, I could shut out the world for a few minutes to release overwhelming moments to the Lord. Settling escalating emotions in this way helped me to regain composure.

Maggie was the first dog we ever crate-trained. We learned that a long, dark-colored blanket draped over the outside of the crate created a private space where she could distance herself safely. When emotions ran high and things got too "people-y" for Maggie, she'd voluntarily retreat to her crate to recover.

When she chose to be alone, we didn't invade her space by going into the crate after her. We trusted that she'd come out again when she was ready. We didn't force her to come close, chase her down, or keep track of her mishaps to remind her of them later.

Other times, when Maggie made mistakes or wasn't sure how to respond, she came straight to me and settled herself on the floor at my feet. Together 24/7, we knew each other well, and the intentions of her heart were beautiful. A gentle caressing touch on her face or ears told her everything was okay.

When there were mishaps, we dealt with those issues as they occurred and kept moving forward. Similarly, God doesn't hold on to our mistakes. Jesus paid our sin debt and set us free (Colossians 2:13-14). There is now, therefore, no condemnation in Christ Jesus (Romans 8:1). He removes our sins as far as the east is from the west (Psalm 103:12), and we are flawless in His sight (Romans 5:1).

God delights in communicating His eternal love for us through our everyday routines and experiences. Through Maggie, I learned to view timeouts differently. Stepping away from stressful moments can allow time for processing big feelings and foster essential recovery as we reposition ourselves at the feet of Christ (Psalm 91:1-6).

It's not God's voice that reminds us of our old sinful nature or past mistakes. We can take those wrong thoughts captive and tell the enemy's voice to be silent, in Jesus' name. God is ever-present. The Author of all creation, He teaches us His love through oft-overlooked things like pets or nature. Jesus never rejected others as too bad, dirty, or too much. His focus was forward, His weapon was love, and His mission was reconciliation.

We choose how we react or respond to the people and world around us. I encourage you to extend grace to yourself and others when you don't handle it well. We handled Maggie's occasional mishaps by spending even more time together and re-training in the areas she was having difficulty. Doing so extended honor, preserved dignity, and reinforced her value as an essential part of our family.

By establishing and fostering a culture of honor in our homes, we create a safe place to learn from mistakes. Vulnerability is essential for growing in love.

Keeping God first in all things allows His voice and presence to be amplified and magnified in our lives.

Scriptures to Ponder

As far as the east is from the west, so far has he removed our transgressions from us. (Psalm 103:12 WEB)

Our faith in Jesus transfers God's righteousness to us and He now declares us flawless in his eyes. (Romans 5:1 TPT)

There is therefore now no condemnation to those who are in Christ Jesus, who don't walk according to the flesh, but according to the Spirit. (Romans 8:1 WEB)

And you who were dead in trespasses and in the uncircumcision of your flesh (your sensuality, your sinful carnal nature), [God] brought to life together with [Christ], having [freely] forgiven us all our transgressions, Having cancelled and blotted out and wiped away the handwriting of the note (bond) with its legal decrees and demands which was in force and stood against us (hostile to us). This [note with its regulations, decrees, and demands] He set aside and cleared completely out of our way by nailing it to [His] cross. (Colossians 2:13-14 AMPC)

Questions for Prayer or Journaling

God does not force His will upon us, and we have free will to accept or reject His invitation to walk with Him. He respects our boundaries, though He wants us to grow in our revelation of His love and mercy. Ask God to show you how He sees you.

We can practice listening to God's voice daily. When was the last time you asked God, "What would You have me do today? What is the adventure You have planned for us today?"

Since God is not focused on our mistakes, we shouldn't be. Ask God to reveal any hidden unforgiveness in your heart towards Him, yourself, or others. When God exposes unforgiveness, we confess what He already knows, repent for agreeing with the enemy's lies and extend forgiveness and blessings in its place. The forgiveness we extend to others is the same release we would want for ourselves (Matthew 6:12).

Let's Pray

Father God, we cannot grasp the vast depths of Your love for us. Like a doting father, You redirect and correct Your wayward children. You bring us to Your saving strength and watch over us like a bodyguard. You lift us up when we're bent over with shame. Transgressions are forgiven through confession and repentance as we boldly come to Your throne of grace (Hebrews 4:15-16). We have freely received the gifts of mercy and forgiveness from You. Teach us to extend the same to others freely. In Jesus' name, we pray. Amen.

Chapter Thirteen

Look and Keep Looking

P rayer meetings were a highlight of our week. Maggie tried hard to remember her "place" sitting on her trusty red fleece blanket but often couldn't hold her excitement and would bolt to the door. Squealing with delight, she'd jump up and down. Some ladies encouraged her jumping, while others extended a "stop" hand signal to show their preference for a calmer greeting.

Maggie took her job as a door greeter seriously and enthusiastically. Once safely inside our home's entry foyer, Maggie eagerly escorted our guests into the living room, welcoming pats on the head and belly rubs.

When meetings started, Maggie would settle down and rest on the floor by my feet, though she preferred to lie on the sofa if there was room. I was in the habit of watching her, especially after the meetings started. Although we had the same core group of ladies who met faithfully, the sessions were open to anyone desiring to join us. Because this was new for us, I wasn't sure how Maggie might react to people coming and going.

The ladies in our prayer group varied in age, ethnicity, and denominational background. As our trust in God and each other grew, we tossed aside our agendas and allowed the Holy Spirit to lead. It was a safe place for challenging our beliefs and exercising our spiritual senses.

We often started our meetings by sharing scriptures or highlights from a recent Sunday message. These God-honoring conversations showed respect for each person's time while allowing latecomers to slip in.

Most often, as I led the group, I sat with my back to the innermost wall of the living room. From this place, I could monitor the front window and door for any visitors who approached. Maggie never missed hearing a car in the driveway or footsteps approaching the door. Did she view it as a party, thinking everyone had come to celebrate her?

Maggie was so much fun, and her reactions were precious. She always perked up when someone approached the house. Her head, eyes, eyebrows, and stringy fur-covered ears lifted instantly in response.

You might argue this next point with me, but I'm convinced that animals see in the spirit realm. God tells us that animals will teach us (Job 12:7), though it's not something I considered before hosting weekly prayer meetings in our home.

During one of our meetings, though no one was there that we could see, Maggie reacted as if someone was coming into the room. Something or someone had captured her attention, but we didn't know what it was. This curious behavior prompted me to ask, "Maggie, what do you see? What are you looking at?"

We soon realized that Maggie was observing spirit-realm activities, angels, or open heavens. She taught us to look, and look again, with the eyes of our hearts (Ephesians 1:18). This behavior also occurred in other settings.

In church or street ministry, Maggie would often growl and resist walking toward anyone manifesting demonically. Spiritual warfare is a topic many churches in America fail to address, but that doesn't change the fact that we're waging war against an invisible enemy.

While I ministered God's healing power through prayer and prophecy, Maggie often positioned herself a few feet away. Because I didn't have any points of reference for what was taking place, I took the matter to God. It surprised me how much He had to say on this topic. A few examples of demonic spirits referenced in the bible are: divination, error, fear, heaviness, and infirmity (Acts 16:16, 1 John 4:6, 2 Timothy 1:7, Isaiah 61:3, Luke 13:11).

There is no magic formula for ministering to others. Each opportunity is as unique as the individual and requires speaking or doing only what you hear and see God saying and doing. Trusting God's lead, a shift in the atmosphere or "knowing" occurs to signal the completion of a ministry session.

By instinct, and without hesitation, after ministering in prayer for healing, Maggie would draw near to the person being ministered to, lovingly and acceptingly placing her head in their hand.

At other times, Maggie would rest or sit in seemingly random locations. Those who exercised their spiritual senses observed and confirmed Maggie was positioning herself in heavenly portals. She'd rest peacefully until the portal closed, moving again to her familiar place by my side.

These experiences strengthened my faith and gave me the courage to travel with God, bringing encounters, healing, and deliverance to others. God was and will always be, the Power source for the wonder of signs and miracles. Still, He allowed Maggie to play an instrumental role in teaching and developing the gifts of the Spirit He placed within me and many others. Indeed, by example, Maggie taught us to look and keep looking.

Scriptures to Ponder

Just ask the animals, and they will teach you. Ask the birds of the sky, and they will tell you. (Job 12:7 NLT)

Open my eyes, that I may see wondrous things out of your law. (Psalm 119:18 WEB)

Moreover Yahweh's word came to me, saying, "Jeremiah, what do you see?" I said, "I see a branch of an almond tree." (Jeremiah 1:11 WEB)

Then one like the appearance of a man touched me again, and he strengthened me. (Daniel 10:18 WEB)

...having the eyes of your hearts enlightened, that you may know what is the hope of his calling, and what are the riches of the glory of his inheritance in the saints, (Ephesians 1:18 WEB)

Questions for Prayer or Journaling

Hebrews 5:14 tells us, "...solid food is for those who are full grown, who by reason of use have their senses exercised to discern good and evil," (WEB). What are some ways you practice exercising your spiritual senses?

In Matthew 15:22, a woman pleads with Jesus to help her demon-possessed daughter; in Mark 9:17, a man brings his son to the disciples for healing from an evil spirit. The great commission given by Jesus to all believers includes casting out demons in His name (Mark 16:17). How did people living thousands of years ago recognize evil spirits? This question prompted me to seek answers from the Bible. With over 600 scripture references on this topic, *Spirit World Truths from God's Word* is an invaluable resource.

What are your beliefs about animals seeing in the spirit realm?

Have you ever sensed an open heaven? Praise and thanksgiving seem to increase our heart's sensitivity to His presence. Is there a song in your heart for Him?

Let's Pray

Father God, let our praises draw us closer to You. Your countless expressions of love far exceed our expectations. We dance in the rivers that overflow from Your throne room. Holy Spirit, fill us with Your Living Waters. A new song rises within us as we think about how You break through for us. Activate the depths of Your love within us, enabling us to serve You and others in a way that glorifies Your name in all the earth. It's in the all-sufficient name of Jesus we pray. Amen.

Chapter Fourteen

"That's not yours."

Maggie's first trainer recommended using a 15-foot retractable leash for our walks. Trusting her advice, we purchased the leash, but it didn't quite work out as we had hoped.

Squirrels, rabbits, and cats can easily distract most dogs, and Maggie was no different. The day she shot out like a rocket to the end of that leash while chasing a squirrel was memorable because she took my shoulder with her. The resulting injury required months of physical therapy to restore muscle strength and range of motion. Through it all, I learned a lot of new things.

I didn't stop walking Maggie; however, I knew we wouldn't be using that retractable leash again. The trainer gave good advice, but we needed another option. To guard my shoulders against further injury, I purchased a much shorter, sturdier leash; and secured that leash to my belt. A rarely recognized benefit of having large, sturdy hips is the power of staying grounded. This excellent option meant Maggie's impulses never swayed me again!

We also practiced a new training command. If I spotted a potential distraction on our walk, I'd say, "Leave it. That's not yours." These words calmed Maggie immediately, allowing us to continue our walk.

My physical therapy appointments were scheduled for six months in a medical facility next to a national historical cemetery. If you are sensitive to the spirit realm, an environment like this can be a lot to filter, primarily if you haven't yet been taught how to handle those situations- and I hadn't. It was all still very new to me.

On one particular visit, the atmosphere suddenly shifted as I walked toward the medical facility and was overcome with despair. I was instantly distraught, filled with anxiety and fear. A steady stream of tears flowed down my cheeks as I gasped for breath. My mind raced. *What was this, and who should I call for help?*

It was frightening! However, everything changed when I heard the Holy Spirit whisper, *This is not yours.*

God was encouraging me to be alert to my surroundings. He invited me to partner with Him in prayer to stand against the negative spirits I was discerning in the atmosphere. This lesson helped shape my walk as a prophetic intercessor.

Jesus is our First Responder in all situations. We can call on Him day or night. Jesus tells us if we follow Him, we will not walk in darkness but have the Light of life (John 8:12 WEB). We can dispel any darkness or negativity in the atmosphere by declaring an opposite spirit, aligned with God's word and in Jesus' name.

What do we do with worldly burdens that are not ours? God invites us to "leave it" at the cross, where we can exchange old for new. When our hearts and hands are full of God's love, we can shine light in dark places and release the peace and love of Christ everywhere we go.

This remembrance came to mind as I walked with Maggie one sunny May day several years later. A squirrel sitting in the road, waving its tail like a flag, might have injured both of us when Maggie was a puppy, but we grew to trust each other. I said, "That's not yours," and we walked right past it as if it wasn't even there.

In all things, we're learning to keep our eyes on Jesus; cutting off the distractions of this world. What God brings to our attention in prayer is part of an intimate relationship with the King of Love. These ongoing conversations allow us to co-labor with God to facilitate change on the earth. We can choose to speak life-giving words (Proverbs 18:21). My friends, the Lord is more fully committed to our success than we can imagine or comprehend on this side of heaven!

Scriptures to Ponder

Only be strong and very courageous. Be careful to observe to do according to all the law which Moses my servant commanded you. Don't turn from it to the right hand or to the left, that you may have good success wherever you go. (Joshua 1:7 WEB)

Then you will call upon Me, and you will come and pray to Me, and I will hear and heed you. Then you will seek Me, inquire for, and require Me [as a vital necessity] and find Me when you search for Me with all your heart. (Jeremiah 29:12-13 AMPC)

For whom he foreknew, he also predestined to be conformed to the image of his Son, that he might be the firstborn among many brothers. Whom he predestined, those he also called. Whom he called, those he also justified. Whom he justified, those he also glorified. (Romans 8:29-30 WEB)

Questions for Prayer or Journaling

We can talk with God about anything, but we must train ourselves to listen for His reply. Would you be willing to walk away or lay things down if you heard Him say, "That's not yours"?

Are there any distractions in your life preventing you from reaching your goals? What needs to happen for you to regain focus? What's one thing you might do differently?

Read Proverbs 18:21 from your favorite Bible or app. Ask God if there have been any situations where your words have not accurately reflected His nature or character. If so, you can repent and make new declarations aligned with God's word! What would He have you pray or declare instead?

Let's Pray

Father God, thank You for teaching us to keep our eyes and thoughts on You. Lord, when we're tempted to chase after the things of this world, You always make a better way. You guard us with Your presence. Our faith is unwavering, and our confidence and trust are in You alone. Thank You for Your precious corrections that restore peace to every area of life. In the mighty name of Jesus, we pray. Amen.

Image copyrighted by Sallie Dawkins. All rights reserved.

Chapter Fifteen

The God Who Sees

Early one spring morning, we heard men's voices in the distance as we navigated our familiar walking path. Border collies are sensitive to noise and alert to passersby or other movements. Dense fog surrounded us that day, and Maggie's short legs hindered her view, yet she remained attentive to her surroundings.

We frequently encountered people walking or riding bicycles. Still, on that day, two men were having a loud conversation while jogging nearby. Stopping to allow them to run past us, Maggie instinctively stood at full attention, her front leg pointing toward the sound of the fast-approaching men.

"It's okay," I said.

Usually acknowledging her concerns with, "It's okay," calmed her, but she wouldn't let it go on this day. Maggie didn't move and held her militant point, continuing to gaze forward.

"It's okay," I repeated, with no change in her behavior.

Perplexed, I wondered if Maggie perceived the men as a threat. Even after they ran past us, she held her point. I didn't share her same concerns, but I wanted to acknowledge her reaction and honor her desire to keep me safe. Pausing for a moment to think of a different way to phrase, "It's okay," I finally blurted out, "I see it. I see these men."

Maggie instantly released her pointer stance and eagerly turned her face toward me. As her big brown eyes locked with mine, I responded with a reassuring smile and a gentle pat on her head. We could then complete our walk. This experience was so unusual that I knew God's hand was in it, but what was He teaching me?

Was my behavior toward God similar? How often had I been frozen in place, refusing to move forward? How often had my limited perspectives prevented me from seeing God's bigger picture? Perhaps I was aware of a change but didn't yet have peace or clarity. I could trust God during those times, but would I?

Fears of failure, rejection, or learning new things (like technology) can evoke a deer-in-the-headlights response from us, leaving us feeling like we've been left behind. That's the enemy attempting to separate us from the love of God. The Lord is our Shepherd (Psalm 23), and He will not move forward without us.

More than anything, I sensed it was a timely reminder that God is seated in heavenly places (Ephesians 2:6). From that elevation, He sees all things. Nothing takes Him by surprise. It is comforting when God acknowledges our concerns and responds, *It's okay. I see what's going on.*

In Genesis 16, God saw Hagar's mistreatment and heard her words of affliction from the wilderness, yet, He directed her to return to Sarai. Sometimes it feels like our world is falling apart, but we can trust God is working to bring our lives into greater alignment. With our eyes fixed on Jesus, we're freed from fears and distractions to run with endurance the race set before us (Hebrews 12:1-2).

Father God's voice is a sweet reassurance that we're safe, even when we can't see through the fogginess of our earthbound existence.

Scriptures to Ponder

So she called the name of Yahweh who spoke to her, "You are El-Roi," for she said, "Here I have seen after he who sees me." (Genesis 16:13 LEB)

The Lord is watching everywhere and keeps his eye on both the evil and the good. (Proverbs 15:3 TLB)

From the place where he lives he looks carefully at all the earth's inhabitants. (Psalm 33:14 NET)

… and raised us up with him, and made us to sit with him in the heavenly places in Christ Jesus, (Ephesians 2:6 WEB)

Questions for Prayer or Journaling

Lord, in which areas of life are my viewpoints obstructed?

Jesus, is there anything hindering my heart from fully receiving the abundance of Your love?

Father God, am I reacting in fear or worry towards anything? How do You see that situation?

Lord, I trust You see all things and will use them for my good, even if it doesn't make sense to me. How can I attach my faith to Your Word and promises in this situation?

Let's Pray

Thank You, Father, for reminding me You are a God of seeing. Indeed, Your Name is El Roi, the God who sees. Your eyes are everywhere, always searching. Nothing is hidden from You, and nothing is impossible for You. Thank You, Lord, that I am secure in You; and that You're always with me. I release, now, all worries, cares, and stress. I receive Your perfect peace that passes all understanding (Philippians 4:7). When I can't see clearly, help me keep my eyes fixed on You. I praise You. In Jesus' name, I pray. Amen.

Image copyrighted by Sallie Dawkins. All rights reserved.

Chapter Sixteen

A Hard Restart

When the Lord asked me to sell my house, He also asked me to place everything on the altar of sacrifice. *Wait, what?*

By that point in my walk with God, I had learned to find comfort in obscure directions like this because it confirmed I wasn't listening to my ego or the enemy's voice. It also forced me to read the Bible to find out what God was saying.

In Exodus 25 and 26, God gave Moses the blueprint for the Tabernacle of His Presence. The altar of sacrifice was in the outer courts of the Tabernacle. It couldn't be bypassed by those in Priestly service who expected to find themselves in God's presence.

What was God asking of me? Over the next several weeks, He was clear. He asked me to give Him the house, furnishings, cars, ministry, relationships, everything familiar—including Maggie.

At the time, it sure felt like I was being punished, but now I see part of the bigger picture. After seventeen years in the same house, I would have been perfectly happy to stay there for the rest of my life. I was comfortable there, and our home-based ministry was fruitful. Still, I said *yes* to God and started the downsizing process.

Maggie moved with me to the next location as I waited to hear the unfolding of God's plan for our lives. Maggie didn't know anything about the altar of sacrifice, but honestly, it distanced my heart from her.

Relief came several months later as I walked with Maggie early one morning through a friend's frost-covered field. God's words came loud and clear to my spirit; *Maggie is yours to keep.* I burst out crying. I hadn't realized until that moment how great the stress of not knowing had been. With this release, we could finally move forward. Holding my breath for months, it suddenly felt safe to breathe, hope, and dream again.

While staying in my previous home would have been comfortable, my time and finances were stretched thin in that location. Staying there would have limited my spiritual growth. I would have missed out on the many new connections, resources, and opportunities the Lord had planned.

God knows our needs and may pick us up and move us to a new place, or He might lovingly, yet firmly, redirect us to a better location. He might also correct our emotions, heart attitudes, thoughts, words, actions, relationships, or limiting stronghold beliefs—all for our benefit, growth, and protection.

Scriptures to Ponder

God saw everything that he had made, and, behold, it was very good. (Genesis 1:31 WEB)

See the birds of the sky, that they don't sow, neither do they reap, nor gather into barns. Your heavenly Father feeds them. Aren't you of much more value than they? (Matthew 6:26 WEB)

Don't forget to show hospitality to strangers, for in doing so, some have entertained angels without knowing it. Remember those who are in bonds, as bound with them, and those who are ill-treated, since you are also in the body. (Hebrews 13:2-3 WEB)

And the world passes away and disappears, and with it the forbidden cravings (the passionate desires, the lust) of it; but he who does the will of God and carries out His purposes in his life abides (remains) forever. (1 John 2:17 AMPC)

Beloved, let's love one another, for love is of God; and everyone who loves has been born of God, and knows God. (1 John 4:7 WEB)

Questions for Prayer or Journaling

We can never be sure what's on the other side of our *yes* to God, but we can trust He wants the best for us. Has God ever asked you to place the individual components of your life on His altar of sacrifice? Do you have a testimony of trusting God through difficult transitions?

In John 13:38 (WEB), Jesus asked Simon Peter, "Will you lay down your life for me?" Is there anything in this world you might have difficulty letting go of or trusting God to hold? What does this reveal about your heart?

In John 10:27, Jesus tells us His sheep hear His voice. He knows us, and we follow Him. While God's voice might be audible, it's most often a quiet inner voice that brings peace. What is God speaking to you?

Let's Pray

Father God, open the ears of our hearts to hear from You. We desire to be so close to You we can listen to Your heartbeat. We cry out to You for help and thank You for answering us with wisdom, blueprints, and strategies for moving forward in every season of life. Lord, grant freedom from the bondage of uncertainty and breathe on us afresh. Restore hope. Strengthen us to resist every subtle form of worry. Lord, You are great and greatly to be praised. In Jesus' name, amen.

Chapter Seventeen

Wisdom Keeps You

Although the Lord had invited me to travel through the eastern portion of our nation to pray, I initially resisted His calling. After all, state borders and businesses were shutting down. I was among the many U.S. residents who voluntarily sheltered in place during the Covid pandemic of 2020. *Did I really need to go out? Couldn't I pray from home?*

These worldly justifications exposed a lack of trust in God. By then, Maggie and I had clocked over 2,500 days of walking and talking with God, which should have prepared us for anything.

Our next adventure with God lasted for about six months. During that time, Maggie and I traveled by car through sixteen states, allowing God's voice to direct our path. Starting in Kentucky, we traveled through Tennessee, the Carolinas, Georgia, and Florida. We traveled through Cape Canaveral, Atlanta, Huntsville, and Meridian on our way to Vicksburg, Dallas, Enid, Kansas City, St. Louis, and other locations. It was a set-apart time requiring immediate obedience as I learned to hear and discern the Lord's voice with increased clarity.

Southerners are well known for their hospitality and generosity. While the southern United States is a beautiful territory, one must also be aware of fire ants, mosquitoes, and armadillos. Our last trip south had been several years earlier and during October—a vastly different experience from the sweltering dog days of summer in which we now traveled.

Maggie had lived most of her life in southern Illinois and thrived in cooler temperatures. We'd laugh our heads off, watching her hop like a bunny through fresh snow drifts. Snow days were nothing but sweet dreams now as the waves of heat and humidity took their toll on both of us.

Maggie needed to stretch after being confined to the relatively small back seat space for hours. When we stopped for the night at a small roadside hotel near Meridian, Maggie was uncharacteristically bossy.

Eager to explore, Maggie found the assigned pet space more than fascinating, though I didn't join her excitement. She leaned hard on the leash, fully determined to sniff every single blade of grass in the designated dog walk area. I couldn't tolerate this behavior, but not for the reason you might be thinking.

Maggie had never encountered fire ants before, but I had. Their distinctive dome-shaped mounds spotted the area resembling a severe case of chicken pox. Fire ants swarm to defend their queen when their home is disturbed, and their stings leave giant blisters you won't soon forget.

The art of whistling eluded me, so instead, Maggie learned to respond when I snapped my fingers. I could have let Maggie have her way when she pulled on the leash, but because I love her, I corrected her and pointed her to a different location.

Skilled dog trainers taught us to redirect naughty behavior, immediately removing access to whatever Maggie was after. On the rare occasion when snapping and pointing didn't work to divert Maggie's attention, I'd grab the handles on her harness to physically remove her from an area. She hated that option!

Fire ants are notoriously hostile, and I didn't want to stir them up unnecessarily. Here, Maggie was leaning on her own understanding (Proverbs 3:5), unaware of hidden potential dangers. Reflecting on this, I asked God if there were any times I behaved similarly toward Him.

While navigating new seasons or territories, we may be unaware of potential harm. We can move forward headstrong, determined to have our way, but God will correct us because He loves us. He corrects us to improve us, teach us, and help us. A good father doesn't want to see his child harmed and will do whatever it takes to keep his child safe. How much more will God our Father do to protect His beloved sons and daughters?

You might wonder, as I once did, *How do we look to see God?* The Lord is always with us. He promises we will find Him when we seek Him wholeheartedly (Jeremiah 29:13). Our Creator God is as near to us as the air we breathe. Those who dare to linger in the stillness of His presence will hear Him. Studying His Word helps us grow confident that we're hearing Him.

Maggie and I were on the same team and counted on each other at home or on the road. She trusted my corrections were for her good. Similarly, Christians are part of God's family, and we can trust His corrections will keep us from harm. According to Proverbs 3:13-14, God's wisdom is pure and more valuable than gold. Wisdom keeps us and preserves the life of those who have it (Ecclesiastes 7:12 WEB).

Scriptures to Ponder

He will not let you stumble; the one who watches over you will not slumber. (Psalm 121:3 NLT)

Yahweh, keep me from the hands of the wicked. Preserve me from the violent men who have determined to trip my feet. (Psalm 140:4 WEB)

Don't forsake her, and she will preserve you. Love her, and she will keep you. (Proverbs 4:6 WEB)

Furthermore, we had the fathers of our flesh to chasten us, and we paid them respect. Shall we not much rather be in subjection to the Father of spirits, and live? (Hebrews 12:9 WEB)

But if any of you lacks wisdom, let him ask of God, who gives to all liberally and without reproach, and it will be given to him. (James 1:5 WEB)

Questions for Prayer or Journaling

Do you lean on your understanding or seek God's direction in a new environment?

Do you trust that God's heart is for you and that His corrections keep you safe and help you prosper?

Do you have questions that require wisdom? Is there a proverb that speaks to this? Have you sought God, or godly counsel, on the matter?

Is there any area of your heart or life off-limits to God? Do you welcome and honor His corrections?

Let's Pray

Father God, we thank You for the vastness of Your mercies toward us. Forgive us for times of ingratitude, murmuring, and complaining. Forgive us for rebelling against You, demanding our way, and agreeing with unsubmissive spirits. You are God Most High, and You alone hold all authority (Ephesians 1:21). Lord, we choose to align our will with Yours and to live in oneness and harmony with You and others. We declare Your Lordship over every area of our lives. May all we do and say be for Your glory, honor, and praise. In Jesus' name, we pray. Amen.

Chapter Eighteen

Trusting God

We were definitely "homebodies" until the Lord called us to travel extensively. No one ever accused me of having a keen sense of navigation, and Maggie wasn't fond of traveling in the car, either. Even riding in the car the few miles to the veterinarian's office would make Maggie sick. Although symptoms lessened as she matured, she didn't fully outgrow this. Therefore, our traveling pace was unhurried. Maggie seemed to do better with the radio off and enjoyed frequent stops for stretching and walking.

The back seat was Maggie's domain; she had access to snacks and water, her best toys, and her favorite blankets. Still, riding in a car for six to eight hours a day, then staying overnight in hotels, took some getting used to.

On this day, outdoor temperatures were well over 100 degrees, and my car's air conditioning unit struggled to keep up. By early afternoon, I could tell Maggie needed a break from the heat, so we checked into the nearest hotel to rest and cool off.

As we sat on the bed in the air-conditioned hotel room, I could hear squeaking wheels outside our door. I didn't think anything of it. When we arrived, I had already noticed the cleaning cart parked at the end of the hallway. However, the unfamiliar noise concerned Maggie. The hair on her neck and shoulders stood on end as she lifted her head to look at me.

I could hear voices in the hallway and knew it must be the cleaning staff. Not having this same measure of comprehension, Maggie mumbled. A little growl formed in her throat. I hushed her, but she barked and then looked straight at me.

I could tell from the quizzical look on her tilted head that my reaction, or lack of it, confused her.

Why wasn't I bothered? Why wasn't I up doing something about this weird sound? Why was I shushing her—telling her to be quiet?

Maggie was rightly concerned about that unfamiliar place. She grumbled, growled, barked, and kept looking at my face. I wasn't reacting to the situation in the way she expected. Why? Because I understood what was happening behind the scenes (on the other side of that closed door), and I knew we need not worry.

Even while I was shushing her, she instinctively scooted in closer. Maggie's heart was beautiful, and she worked hard to please others, bringing tremendous joy to the lives of many. Lightly stroking the fur on her back, I assured her everything was okay and that she could rest. A few moments later, she licked my hand, laid her head down, and closed her eyes.

In an instant, I knew God was speaking through the situation. I can get upset about silly things I don't know anything about. I may mumble and grumble and alert Him to it because I'm sure He's not seeing what I see or hearing what I hear! That's not true, though. Even amid the storm, Jesus slept in the boat (Matthew 8:24). That He wasn't worried does not mean He wasn't interested or concerned. The Lord cares about the things that concern us.

I was correcting the dog, but God was correcting me. He knows everything, and we can trust Him. We need only to keep our eyes on Him and look to Him for our instructions, provision, and comfort. This lesson reminded me that God's got it. My job is to abide in Him and rest with my head on His shoulder (John 13:23). My job is to listen and stay in tune with the heartbeat of God.

When the cart returned down the hallway a second time, Maggie opened her eyes and grumbled again. This time, I responded differently as she looked straight into my face. Honoring her need to be seen, heard, and known, I acknowledged the sound by turning my head toward the door before responding, "I hear it. You're okay." These words brought instant comfort, and no further action was required. Within a few moments, she was fast asleep.

Scriptures to Ponder

For as the heavens are higher than the earth, so are my ways higher than your ways, and my thoughts than your thoughts. (Isaiah 55:9 WEB)

Trust in him at all times, you people. Pour out your heart before him. God is a refuge for us. Selah. (Psalm 62:8 WEB)

"Come to me, all you who labor and are heavily burdened, and I will give you rest." (Matthew 11:28 WEB)

One of his disciples, whom Jesus loved, was at the table, leaning against Jesus' breast. (John 13:23 WEB)

For as the sufferings of Christ abound to us, even so our comfort also abounds through Christ. (2 Corinthians 1:5 WEB)

Questions for Prayer or Journaling

Do you trust God with all things or only some things? Invite the Comforter to minister to you today.

Do you only pray when there are problems, or are you intentional about spending time with God and asking Him how you can minister to Him?

When was the last time you sat before the Lord in silence?

Imagine your head resting on Jesus. Like John, you are the disciple whom Jesus loves. Living this close to God causes all our worries to fall away. How would living from this safe place of His presence change your life?

Read Psalm 2 from your favorite Bible or app. God sits in heaven and laughs, but we are seated in heavenly places with Him (Ephesians 1:3). Ask God to show you why He's laughing and journal His response.

Let's Pray

Father God, we praise Your beautiful name! Your words are our firm foundation. The storms of life do not toss us about. Your love gives us triumph over every scheme of the enemy. We don't need to fear a thing (Luke 12:7)! No harm will come to us. You hear our cries for help and protect us. We're confident of Your love and choose to rest in the safety of Your arms of faithfulness. In Jesus' name, we pray. Amen.

Image copyrighted by Sallie Dawkins. All rights reserved.

Chapter Nineteen

The Dog Church

An out-of-town missionary friend prompted a visit to the Cane Ridge Meeting House.[1] Cane Ridge, in Paris, Kentucky, was one location of the second Great Revival in the United States. According to historical markers, Presbyterians constructed the original log meeting house in 1791. The Great Revival began in 1799, but came to Kentucky in 1801, resulting in thousands of early settlers and pioneers of all faiths receiving salvation over the next few decades.

As we toured the premises, we discovered they had encased the original log meeting house in a stone structure to preserve its integrity and significance. A museum on the property paid tribute to the host of the early revivals. It caused us to wonder, where was God in all this?

My friend and I walked the property, prayed blessings upon the territory, then stopped at a picnic table to have communion and write in our journals as we talked with God. While Cane Ridge was undoubtedly fascinating, it couldn't compare with what God had planned for us later in the day. If you've ever wondered what it's like to live life yielded to God's adventures, you'll love this next part of the story.

A subtle stirring of the Holy Spirit caused an abrupt halt to our drive home. Right in the middle of our conversation, I felt God leading me to stop at a location on the other side of the highway. This divinely inspired U-turn took place in Hopewell, Kentucky.

According to a nearby historical marker, we were standing in front of the Hopewell Presbyterian Church, founded in 1787. That made the Hopewell Church a few years older than the Cane Ridge location we'd just visited.

About a minute later, a car pulled up, and the driver motioned for us to come close. The woman introduced herself as Clara and explained that she lived nearby. She asked if we had come to visit "the dog church."

I explained we were intercessory missionaries visiting the area. Though I felt God redirecting us to the church, I didn't know why and certainly didn't know anything about a dog church. My friend Mary Beth and I both looked at each other and laughed. Only God could do something like this.

Clara explained that Hopewell Church's commitment was to honor the earth and all God's creatures by allowing families to bring pets to Sunday services.[2] She and her adult son, John, had been on their way to lunch when they spotted our car in the driveway.

We appreciated Clara's thoughtful invitation to walk through their new prayer garden. That would have been more than gracious, but she then encouraged us to go inside the church to pray and trusted us with the building's keys! The contrast between this experience and the one we just left at Cane Ridge was stark!

While both locations held historical significance, one was closed in and overgrown, while the other remained open and inviting. One place emphasized those hosting our nation's revival, and the other hosted the manifest presence of the One True Living God.

While praying, I told my friend that I felt God had meant for us to pray for Clara, and she agreed. Thinking we had missed the opportunity, it delighted us when Clara and John returned about twenty minutes later. Clara shared that when they arrived at the restaurant, she felt a stirring within her from the Holy Spirit to drive back to the church to ask us to pray for John's healing.

The hand and voice of God had been so subtle that day I nearly missed Him guiding me to take a detour. Clara and her son also could have ignored the Spirit's unction to turn around. After all, they were already at the restaurant.

God rewarded our obedience, and we hosted His presence and power to release healing and speak prophetically into this family's destiny. Though I had never ministered alongside Mary Beth before, her gifts and mine flowed in a way that left us all glorifying God. His presence there was tangible.

Because dogs were welcome in that place, I detached Maggie's leash and allowed her to roam while we prayed for John's healing. He said he felt the results immediately. Though Maggie initially avoided John, after our prayer time, she approached him voluntarily, placing her head in his hand. She remained close to John as we marveled at God's loving presence in that place.

More than training, Maggie had a natural affinity for healing ministry. Never overstepping boundaries, she taught me how important it was to remain faithful to my calling. Each member of the body has a unique role. On this day, it was like a divine dance as my friend Mary Beth and I trusted God's leading in the gifts of the Spirit. God's love and faithfulness manifested as He activated our gifts to provide what His body needed!

Scriptures to Ponder

In that day I will restore the fallen house of David. I will repair its damaged walls. From the ruins I will rebuild it and restore its former glory. (Amos 9:11 NLT)

Howbeit when he, the Spirit of truth, is come, he will guide you into all truth: for he shall not speak of himself; but he shall hear, that shall he speak: and he will shew you things to come. (John 16:13 KJV)

"Stretch out your hand with healing power; may miraculous signs and wonders be done through the name of your holy servant Jesus." (Acts 4:30 NLT)

But ye have an unction from the Holy One, and ye know all things. (1 John 2:20 KJV)

But the anointing which ye have received of him abideth in you, and ye need not that any man teach you: but as the same anointing teacheth you of all things... (1 John 2:27 KJV)

Questions for Prayer or Journaling

Have you ever felt an unction of the Holy Spirit? What did that feel like, and what was God prompting you to say or do in that instance?

Successful ministry to others requires a complete yielding to God. The outcome can get muddied when ego leads. Do you have a testimony of sharing the pure Living Water of God with others? Do you have a "dirty water" testimony you've learned from?

Read James 2:19 from your favorite Bible or app. The demons believe there is One God, do you?

Let's Pray

Father God, my heart desires to live fully yielded to You. Use me to do Your will on earth. Purify my heart to administer Your healing power to others in truth and love. Holy Spirit, I desire to grow in sensitivity to Your presence and leading. I'm sorry for failing to acknowledge or knowingly resist You. Please forgive me for the times I followed men rather than You. I purpose to love You with all my heart, soul, mind, and strength (Mark 12:30). Help me fulfill this purpose. It's in the marvelous name of Jesus, I pray. Amen.

---

1. https://www.hopewellmuseum.org/learn/historic-preservation/bourbon-county-historical-markers/cane-ridge-meetinghouse/
2. https://www.hopewellmuseum.org/learn/historic-preservation/bourbon-county-historical-markers/hopewell-church/

Chapter Twenty

Saying Goodbye

M aggie passed away too soon, leaving a "loyal till the end" legacy. Her final year of life was plagued with various health issues. The official diagnosis of hemangiosarcoma (HSA) came a week after undergoing emergency surgery to remove her tumor-filled spleen.

Something had been off for months. The spirit of death was on her, and I commanded it to go, in Jesus' name. I did everything I knew to do. I know my authority in Christ (Mark 16:17-18). I rebuked that spirit, yet it wouldn't leave. Every day, I declared healing, wholeness, and good health over Maggie. I pleaded the Blood of Jesus over her. I didn't understand why this was happening or why God seemingly wasn't answering our prayers.

Maggie had been seen at an emergency animal care facility when she started having bloody stools. During Covid, veterinarian services were in unusually high demand. When her regular doctor nor the backup emergency veterinarian had any openings, I made an appointment with a clinic in a neighboring town. There, she received prescriptions for antibiotics and pain. Lab results were consistently negative for diabetes, but no one seemed to pinpoint the root of the actual problem.

We had already tried two different antibiotics that month. With no noticeable improvement, I called Maggie's regular veterinarian, Dr. Melonie, to make an appointment. Five days later, they still suspected a possible back injury. On this visit, Maggie was severely dehydrated, and her urine was dark brown. An x-ray revealed Maggie's spine was perfectly intact, but an enormous mass in her abdomen was of concern. Dr. Melonie suggested an ultrasound for clarity.

With their schedule booked for the next several hours, they told me to leave Maggie there and that they'd call me afterward to pick her up. Stooping to Maggie's eye level, I said, "Maggie, these people are going to help you," then whispered, "Jesus is coming back soon, and so am I. I'll see you soon." Always charging to be by my side, this time Maggie didn't resist or pull on the leash as I walked away. It was a precursor sign things might be far worse than we imagined.

Several hours later, Dr. Melonie called with the results of the ultrasound. Maggie had tumors in her spleen. With my consent, they would operate immediately. An expanding spleen added pressure to the chest and explained Maggie's increasingly labored breathing.

Maggie's spleen and tumors weighed over two pounds. In comparison, an average human spleen weighs just seven ounces. IV fluids and antibiotics given after the surgery aided Maggie's recovery. Although she was up walking around later that day, she refused to eat or drink anything post-op.

The assistant said every time they encouraged her to walk around outside; Maggie looked all over the parking lot for my car. She missed me, and I missed her. They wanted to keep her for observation longer, but after three days of not eating, they called me to come to get her.

Stopping by my dad's house, Maggie made me a liar when I told my dad she probably wouldn't eat or drink anything. She quickly gobbled almost half a can of dog food. Except for being partly shaved and having her front leg wrapped in bandages, you would have never known she'd just had major surgery. Maggie seemed glad to be home.

We returned to the vet the following day to have the catheter extracted, and Maggie's health steadily improved over the next several days. The day before she died, my dad and I had laughed over how much fun she was having with her favorite squeaky ball.

Everything changed overnight.

Less than 24 hours earlier, I had stood in the kitchen of our home talking with Dr. Melonie by speakerphone. Maggie rested in her crate a few feet away. The pathologist's report had just come in. "It's an aggressive form of cancer of the blood vessels. Dogs diagnosed with HSA might expect to live six to twelve months. I could refer her to chemotherapy treatments, but it's expensive, and the results aren't guaranteed. Or you could wait it out and let it run its course."

Expenses didn't matter; we were more concerned with her quality of life. Maggie was due to have her stitches removed in another week. After that, if she felt well enough, we might go on a road trip to see family. We would do whatever it took to make her last few months enjoyable.

We went outside around 3:30 the following morning. Everything seemed fine as we walked back into the house. Maggie went straight to her crate, but I had a quick "thought" to scoop her up and carry her upstairs, so I did that. It would be easier to monitor her needs if she slept upstairs. Covering the bed with a clean sheet, we made room for Maggie.

We settled in, but Maggie started throwing up about an hour later. She continued throwing up off and on for the next few hours. Mama-instinct kicked in as I cleaned her with a warm washcloth and changed the bedding. I did this three more times before daylight.

At the first morning light, I realized how critical her condition was. Tense and heavy, Maggie was now fully paralyzed—it was a shock for both of us. I cried to God, "Lord, this wasn't six or twelve months! It hasn't even been a full day yet. Not *one* day!"

Carefully wrapping Maggie in the sheet, I raced downstairs to call the veterinarian's office. *Were they even open yet?* Wild-eyed, Maggie struggled to breathe. When the technician answered the phone, I said, "Tell Dr. Melonie, 'It's time.' She'll know what that means." The assistant relayed the message but notified me that Dr. Melonie was prepping for surgery. It would be hours before they could fit us into their busy schedule.

Did Maggie have hours left?

She lost control of her bowels while I was holding her. Maggie's breathing was shallow, and her tongue had already turned blue when we arrived at Dr. Melonie's office. An assistant ushered us into an exam room, where I gently laid Maggie on the table. My beloved companion took her last breath a few moments later.

To say I wrestled with God over this loss is a gross understatement. My heart couldn't reconcile

Maggie's sudden death. Though it sure felt like I was being punished and rejected, those feelings weren't true. I didn't understand why this had happened. I had more questions than answers. *Why wasn't Maggie healed? Had she been a crutch? Had I grown to depend on her for things I should have been looking to God for? Was she keeping me from walking in the fullness of my God-designed destiny? Had the spirit of death that landed on her really come for me?*

This heart wound was raw for several months. Through it all, God exposed lingering sorrow, grief, and sadness of soul. Our God is a good Father and exposes darkness or lack by shining His healing light and abundance of love onto those broken and bruised places (Exodus 15:26, Psalm 103:1-3).

My reaction to Maggie's death revealed an opportunity to grow in faith. This inner struggle proved that the Spirit of God was working within me. When I dared to come close, He invited me to release the weight of this burden to Him. The release I needed finally came through a vision as I stood in the kitchen.

Jesus, my Good Shepherd, called my name and stood with His arms firmly extended, palms up, to receive all I had been unable to release. That's when I looked down and, with my spiritual eyes, noticed my arms extended, holding Maggie's lifeless body. This image revealed my actual heart condition.

My refusal to let go became a burden God never intended. Maggie's death had been added to other unprocessed losses and had grown too heavy for me to carry. We find freedom from the weight of our deepest sorrows by going straight to the Man of sorrows.

> He was despised and rejected and forsaken by men, a Man of sorrows and pains, and acquainted with grief and sickness; and like One from Whom men hide their faces He was despised, and we did not appreciate His worth or have any esteem for Him. (Isaiah 53:3 AMPC)

Tears flowed as I dropped to my knees to kneel before my Lord and King. Jesus received Maggie's lifeless body with profound tenderness and love. Indeed, when we view God as uncaring, we view our Lord through the wrong lenses.

When we draw near to God, He draws near to us (James 4:8). God is not distant. The fullness of our triune God is within every believer. Holding on to Maggie kept my hands too full to accept anything new. The very moment I released Maggie to Jesus, I received supernatural peace.

As much as I loved Maggie and all she represented in my life, I'm assured that Jesus loves her more. I would have loved to have had more years with Maggie, but now I confidently trust that God fulfilled His purpose for her in my life.

Scriptures to Ponder

Yahweh is near to those who have a broken heart, and saves those who have a crushed spirit. (Psalm 34:18 WEB)

He heals the broken in heart, and binds up their wounds. (Psalm 147:3 WEB)

Blessed are those who mourn, for they shall be comforted. (Matthew 5:4 WEB)

Blessed be the God and Father of our Lord Jesus Christ, the Father of mercies and God of all comfort; who comforts us in all our affliction, that we may be able to comfort those who are in any affliction, through the comfort with which we ourselves are comforted by God. (2 Corinthians 1:3-4 WEB)

Questions for Prayer or Journaling

Sickness and disease are not from God and do not bring Him glory. In Exodus 15:26, God refers to Himself as Jehovah Rapha, the God Who Heals. Do you believe in supernatural healing, creative miracles, and resurrection life?

Abrupt endings can leave us wrestling with God for answers as we attempt to reconcile and make sense of what's happening, but does it say we don't trust God?

God's abundant blessings bring peace, safety, contentment, health, prosperity, and completeness. In Mark 10:51, Jesus asked, "What do you want Me to do for you?" How would you answer this question?

Let's Pray

Father God, rejection and abandonment are not from You. Forgive me for the times when I doubted Your love. Holy Spirit, You are my soul's Comforter and faithful Friend. You are concerned about the things that concern me. Thank You for guiding me through dark days of grief and sorrow. God, You are my Great Physician and Prince of Peace. When I push down raw pain and big feelings, You encourage me to unpack them and release them to You. Your exchanges are the best: a crown of beauty for ashes, the oil of joy for mourning, and the garment of praise for despair (Isaiah 61:1-3). Lord, I will trust You, for You alone are good. In Jesus' name I pray. Amen.

Chapter Twenty-One

Maggie's Legacy

As a puppy, Maggie brought high-octane energy to my somewhat dull, predictable life. When Maggie joined our family, her immaturity was evident. To outsiders, I'm sure my spiritual immaturity was just as apparent. After twenty years as a Christian, I still struggled with the foundational concepts of identity and purpose. I share this part of my testimony in The Awakening Christian Series. I marvel at God's strategy for setting Maggie and me on a parallel training course. My corrections of Maggie were often God's corrections toward me.

Legacy is an inheritance we leave for the generations that come after us. Maggie's legacy is one of trust-filled obedience and love-based loyalty. After years of hiding behind walls of self-protection and self-preservation, Maggie was the conduit God used to help me reengage with life. Her companionship gave me the courage to step outside the comfort of my home to experience incredible adventures with God. We walked many miles together, and every step was a victory.

I view life through pictures, with words sometimes lagging. The message was clear when Maggie gently tapped my foot with her paw and then glanced toward her leash hanging by the door—she wanted to go outside. With animals, communication is about more than words. We were two very different creatures, but we eventually learned to communicate effectively and intuitively.

Maggie's abounding enthusiasm created continuing momentum for growing in faith. When I think I'm falling behind in my walk with God, I remind myself that it took three years of daily practice for Maggie and me to master the art of walking in step with each other. Every day I walked with Maggie, I grew more alert to God's faithful presence. These set-apart years were a time of rapid spiritual growth and healing, preparing me for ordination as a healing evangelist.

Perhaps there are some lessons we can only learn through adversity. Distracted and consumed by the tidal wave of emotions tied to Maggie's sudden death, I never thought to ask God what His purpose was. Adversity allows us to see our weaknesses and moves us to a place of grace to receive God's strength (2 Corinthians 13:9-10). Wrestling with God was unnecessary; I only needed to release my burdens to Him. God wants us to bring all things straight to Him. He has grace, peace, and healing for us in the place of sorrow.

Maggie was a genuine gift from God—used by Him in many ordinary yet miraculous ways. Through her eyes, I learned to see the world differently. God was not punishing me with Maggie's death, nor did He snatch her from my hands. These are worldviews, not heavenward views. When Maggie died, I walked away from her lifeless body. I failed to see her death as an opportunity to grow in faith by praying for resurrection life. Although I missed this chance with Maggie, I have since taken advantage of opportunities to pray for resurrection life over other animals. It hasn't happened yet, but I'm still hopeful and determined to keep praying.

Maggie added value to my life and taught me to love and trust others more deeply. Because of Maggie's influence, I grew to trust God's voice, guidance, and corrections. I was never alone walking Maggie—the abiding presence of God was continually with us. In her absence, He is still here.

Maggie's legacy lives on.

Images copyrighted by Sallie Dawkins. All rights reserved.

Ten Fun Facts about Border Collies

1. The word "collie" is most likely a variation of the Scottish *colly* meaning "coal-black."[1] Sheepdogs were called "border" collies because they originated from the border area between Scotland and England.

2. Border Collies are highly intelligent and can learn hundreds of words and commands. AKC Certified Trick Dogs have to respond to 10 advanced tricks.[2]

3. Border Collies are working dogs and happiest when put to work. Maggie could accurately identify and retrieve over 60 different objects or toys. After a while, we started naming her toys after colors to make it easier for us to keep up with them.

4. Border Collies are herding dogs and love to round things up. Maggie never visited

a sheep farm, but she loved to run circles around children!

5. Famous Scottish poet, Robert Burns, owned a Border Collie named Luath. Luath is often featured alongside Burns in statues.[3]

6. Adult Border Collies usually weigh between 30 and 45 pounds, with females weighing less than males.

7. Border Collies have a double coat and need regular grooming to control excessive shedding. Their thick fur also causes them to overheat quickly in hot climates.

8. In the 1995 Oscar-winning movie "Babe," Border Collies taught a pig how to herd sheep for Farmer Hoggett.[4] "Babe" is one of my favorite movies of all time.

9. The most common color for Border Collies is black and white, but they might also be shades of brown and white; black, brown, and white; or have a mottled (merle) coat. Maggie was black, with a pop of white hair on her chest.

10. Border Collies typically live between 12 and 15 years,[5] but Maggie was eight years old when she died. Count me in as part of that group of people who believe all dogs go to

heaven, and we'll be gloriously reunited one day soon.

1. Harper Douglas, "Etymology of collie," Online Etymology Dictionary, accessed January 4, 2023, https://www.etymonline.com/word/collie.
2. https://www.akc.org/sports/trick-dog/
3. https://en.wikipedia.org/wiki/Robert_Burns#/media/File:Robert_Burns_Winthrop_Square.jpg
4. https://www.imdb.com/title/tt0112431/?ref_=tt qt_qt_tt
5. https://en.wikipedia.org/wiki/Border_Collie

Image copyrighted by Sallie Dawkins. All rights reserved.

Dog Training Basics

It's a good thing puppies are so adorable because the investment of time in training them can be pretty substantial. Teaching a puppy new commands requires personal, face-to-face interaction and careful listening. While words and hand signals are initially foreign to dogs, this combination makes learning easier. Commands establish boundaries to maintain safety, communicate consistent expectations, and help build mutual trust.

You can help your puppy or dog learn new commands by offering small treats. Maggie enjoyed all kinds of treats, but we used plain Cheerios™ for teaching her new commands because they were more budget-friendly!

Certified dog trainers use specific commands and signals. Still, many of the commands and hand signals we used with Maggie evolved. Consistency is vital, so use whatever works for you and your dog. Here are a few of the commands we taught Maggie to follow:

Yes! = An affirmative, enthusiastic response that includes a big smile (and sometimes a treat).

No! = This negative response, correction, or redirection might include a stern look or "*Eh!*"

Watch! = Pointing to my eyes as I'd say, "Watch," taught Maggie to make eye contact.

Come! = Clapping twice then extending my right arm straight out at a 90-degree angle drew Maggie near when she was far away.

Go home! or **Crate!** = Usually followed by pointing in that direction, encouraged Maggie to return to a safe place of belonging.

Down! = Pointing downward let Maggie know a passive position was required.

Sit! = Together with a signal showing the back of my hand, Maggie responded by sitting.

Stay! or **Stop!** or **Wait!** = Using a firm "stop" hand signal taught Maggie self-control.

Heel! or **Close!** = Snapping my fingers and pointing straight down encouraged Maggie to come closer while leash walking.

Drop it! or **Take it!** = This one was primarily auditory and signaled to make a trade.

Leave it! or **That's not yours!** = Auditory signal that reinforced boundaries.

Find it! or **Go get it!** = Shrugging my shoulders or asking, "Where's [*specifically named toy*]? was one of Maggie's favorite games.

Image copyrighted by Sallie Dawkins. All rights reserved.

Bible Translations

Unless otherwise indicated, all Scripture quotations are taken from www.BibleGateway.com. This page is a continuation of the Copyright Page.

Scripture quotations taken from the Amplified® Bible (AMP), Copyright © 2015 by The Lockman Foundation. Used by permission. www.lockman.org

Scripture quotations taken from the Amplified® Bible (AMPC), Copyright © 1954, 1958, 1962, 1964, 1965, 1987 by The Lockman Foundation Used by permission. www.lockman.org.

Scripture quotations marked (KJV) taken from the King James Version is Public Domain in the USA.

Scripture quotations marked (LEB) are from the *Lexham English Bible*. Copyright 2012 Logos Bible Software. Lexham is a registered trademark of Logos Bible Software.

Scripture quotations marked (NLT) are taken from the Holy Bible, New Living Translation, copyright ©1996, 2004, 2015 by Tyndale House Foundation. Used by permission of Tyndale House Publishers, Carol Stream, Illinois 60188. All rights reserved.

Scripture quotations marked (TLB) are taken from The Living Bible copyright © 1971. Used by permission of Tyndale House Publishers, Carol Stream, Illinois 60188. All rights reserved.

Scripture quotations marked (MSG) are taken from THE MESSAGE, copyright © 1993, 2002, 2018 by Eugene H. Peterson. Used by permission of NavPress. All rights reserved. Represented by Tyndale House Publishers, Inc.

The Scriptures quoted are from the NET Bible® https://netbible.com copyright ©1996, 2019 used with permission from Biblical Studies Press, L.L.C. All rights reserved.

Scripture quotations marked (TPT) are from The Passion Translation®. Copyright © 2017, 2018 by Passion & Fire Ministries, Inc. Used by permission. All rights reserved. ThePassionTranslation.com.

The World English Bible (WEB) is in the Public Domain. However, "World English Bible" is a Trademark.

About the Author

In 2015, a heart encounter with God challenged Sallie Dawkins' entire belief system and set her on a supernatural journey of discovery that rapidly transformed her life. Sallie believes cultivating a deeper relationship with Jesus brought triumph over decades-long chronic pain. Teaching through testimony, Sallie answers questions Christians can't, don't, or won't ask in church. She shares her breakthrough journey in the #1 bestselling and international award-winning Awakening Christian Series.

Sallie Dawkins is a US-based prophetic intercessor ordained through Joan Hunter Ministries as a healing evangelist. She is passionate about seeing people healed and set free to enjoy abundant life in Christ. Her heart is to show others that they too can triumph over challenges, experience God's miracles in their own lives, and serve as God's couriers to deliver the healing power of Christ's love throughout the earth.

Sallie lives in Kentucky, USA. Learn more at www.SallieDawkins.com.

Did you enjoy this volume of the Open Ark Series? We appreciate feedback, and love hearing what readers have to say. Your input helps to make subsequent versions of this book and future books better. Please leave an honest book review letting us know what you thought of the book. Sharing your favorite quote, a photo, or video makes it even more special!

Animals are incredible companions often used by God to teach powerful Kingdom principles. Do you have an animal testimony you'd like to share? If so, contact us at OpenArkBooks@gmail.com to learn how you can submit your story for possible inclusion in a future edition of the Open Ark Series.